THE STUDENT'S GUIDE TO WORLD THEATRE

The emergence of theatre. A temple stage in Shantung.

THE STUDENT'S GUIDE
TO
WORLD THEATRE

By

E. J. BURTON, M.A.

Illustrated by Diana Quin

LONDON: HERBERT JENKINS

First published by
Herbert Jenkins Ltd.,
3 Duke of York Street,
London, S.W.1
1962

PRINTED IN GREAT BRITAIN BY
BRISTOL TYPESETTING CO. LTD.
BARTON MANOR - ST. PHILIPS
BRISTOL 2

PREFACE

The purpose of this book is to suggest to the student—and indeed all interested in the living theatre—fields of essential study, and to initiate their exploration. Its composition has been guided by the following main considerations :

1. It is desirable that students should learn something of theatre as it exists and develops, not only in their own country but throughout the world. Too many judge by their own limited experience, accepting, for example, the picture-frame presentations of West End successes by the local dramatic society as a theatrical norm. The better such presentations are, within their particular conventions, the less easy is it for a student to recognise other forms of theatre, or even of drama.

2. Those who today argue about problems of theatre, and are concerned with what seems to be its precarious future, should be aware of, or in a position to assess, the nature of their subject, its associated arts, its actual function in the world, its place in varying cultures and societies, and its essential elements, origins and development. Too often we tend to dogmatise about what theatre ought to be according to inner beliefs and wishes formed *without reference to theatre*. We try to impose limitations or pressures from outside on the " thing in itself ", oblivious of its nature and ways of working.

3. Today, we are aware more than before of the importance of cultures other than our own and recognise their achievements. We no longer make our own contemporary British theatre the measure of theatre in other countries, ages, and cultures. In the past, in practice if not in acknowledged theory, we tended to regard our own dramatic activities as the norm, and treated everything else as deviations.

4. The student of theatre should be ready to re-assess his atti-

5

tudes and admit that theatre never was, essentially, and never can be, if it is to survive, what he imagined. Its vitality is drawn from human life and experience through channels, religious and social, which may hardly fit his own preconceived or "logically" established views of life and society. Theatre may change under social pressures. At the same time, it is inspired by individual enthusiasms which draw, somehow, upon hidden emotional (and maybe other) powers within the community. Quin may rebuke the obviously faulty acting of Garrick, who breaks all the accepted rules; yet Garrick revives and uses, as a practical worker in theatre, a great surge of human energy and enthusiasm. Theorists of the eighteenth, or any other century, may tell us what life ought to be, socially, morally, economically; but life is greater than any theories about it. Similarly, we can rarely state our understanding of theatre in definitive terms; we can only note what has been involved and evolved during its development, everywhere and in all ages, whatever apparent divergences and conflicts there may be. Experience teaches, but to state that experience *precisely* is not possible.

5. Influences from other countries have, during the present century, impinged on western theatre, just as in the past one European country influenced another. We are no longer isolated. The nineteenth century tendency for other parts of the world to copy the west is ceasing. Countries with new national pride are more conscious of their own heritage; further, the traffic is two-way; we ourselves are learning from others. It is admittedly difficult to give accurate and up-to-date information on contemporary theatre throughout the world. I have relied first upon my own observation of dramatic performances—specifically, for example, Chinese, Japanese, and to a less degree Indonesian theatre; secondly, on filmed records of rituals, dances, and plays, including Far Eastern puppets and shadow dramas. Further information has been derived from verbal reports given, often, by my own students on drama in localities as remote as Labuan and Mexico. Lastly, I have drawn on eye-witness accounts by other writers, such as those given by Mr. Faubion Bowers in his very valuable *Theatre in the East*. To Mr. Bowers and his publishers, Messrs. Nelson, I am sincerely grateful for permission, so readily given, to use this material.

6. Since drama is produced from communal activities, originating in and utilising the experiences, social and religious

attitudes, of those who engage in it, a short account is provided of the historical backgrounds to its development. Only by familiarising ourselves, so far as we can, with the intentions and assumptions of a performance can we enjoy and appreciate theatre anywhere or of any time.

7. The term " total theatre " is used for a dramatic representation which employs many, or all, of the means of communication at the performers' disposal, not only action, spoken dialogue, and developed décor, but music, song, dance, and whatever stylised conventions or accepted symbolism may further evoke audience response. " Total theatre " is a convenient, if loose, term which alerts the reader or listener to consider the effect of a presentation and the means by which this is achieved. Again, beginners sometimes judge everything from the basis of " naturalism "; all other forms of presentation are to them either " naturalism " with other elements, such as song and dance, intruded, or aberrant from the normal—and not real " theatre ". Hence the use of the term to stress that all these other elements are an integral part of true theatre and themselves truly theatrical. Shakespeare's own practice may serve as a tolerable example of what is meant, even without citing Eastern drama or Western " opera ".

8. Reading lists are added to help the student. These do not contain necessarily final or definitive authorities but rather what we may term " intermediate " books to serve as an introduction to more detailed and advanced studies.

My thanks are due to Miss Diana Quin, who has devised simple diagrammatic illustrations from reliable sources, and to Mrs. Lane, the Librarian at Trent Park College, who has helped me in many ways too numerous to mention.

The illustrations in this book are meant to lead the student on to further study, to more detailed plans and photographs in such books as Allardyce Nicoll's *Development of the Theatre,* Faubion Bowers' *The Japanese Theatre,* or A. C. Scott's *The Classical Theatre of China.* We have tried to indicate such basic considerations as the proximity of temple buildings, the patterns of stage lay-out, the development of dramatic conventions.

Thus, in Chapter I, are shown varying emergences (by contrasting illustrations) of drama from religious rites in paganism, Hinduism, and Christianity. In Chapters II and III the masks of folk drama in Ceylon, mediaeval England and Japan are exemplified. Reference to our list will show that in Chapter VI and VII we set side by side facial make-up and masks from Bali, Rome and the *commedia*. Theatre plans indicate the development and use of differing platforms, the introduction of perspective in the west, and thus, later, the " picture frame ". Such illustrations (which are also grouped according to chapter material) are not ends in themselves but may suggest patterns of theatre practice. Around these the student may form his own judgments, adding to or modifying the simple diagrammatic presentations we have provided.

Since this book went to press, Dr. Richard Southern's *Seven Stages of Theatre* has appeared. In this valuable study Dr. Southern traces, with ample illustration from the past and present dramatic enactments of the world, the pattern of development to be found, identifying seven significant stages in this. His work has especial importance for students interested in the emergence of the actor and the nature and conventions of acting spaces. There is a careful examination of religious presentations (e.g. in Tibet and neighbouring countries) and folk-drama in general.

CONTENTS

9

Contents

Contents

LIST OF LINE ILLUSTRATIONS

THE STUDENT'S GUIDE TO WORLD THEATRE

CHAPTER I

THE EMERGENCE OF THEATRE

1. *Introduction*

On the lawn two kittens are playing. For a while they chase each other, scuffle, roll over, savagely clawing and biting, ears back, eyes dilated—apparently ferocious, terrified, or terrifying, in turn. Yet all the while neither is hurt, the claws are sheathed, and the biting never goes into the flesh. This preliminary dance ended, they go into a more thoughtful series of actions. One scampers away to hide under the rhubarb leaves. From this cool lair, he gazes, crouched against the ground. You can just see his brightly blue kitten eyes and nose tip. Now the other, having nonchalantly (and somewhat clumsily) licked himself, walks delicately towards the rhubarb, ignoring the lurker. As he is about to pass, the other jumps out—but not until the casual passer-by presents the back of his neck to the ambush. With a movement that seems half serpent, half monkey, the stroller whirls (apparently in the air) to meet the attack. Again they scuffle, cuff, and then run off in opposite directions. Soon one again approaches. The actions are resumed—hunt, ambush, attack, tip-toe stalking, hiding, tracking.

All the time they are learning, developing, rehearsing. Soon they will be hunting, stalking, springing on the prey in reality—and displaying their first trophies, the mouse ceremonially laid on the doorstep, or even a young rabbit. The " imaginative " play, the pretended actions, events, situations, gradually extend the power and self-fulfilment (one might say self-expression) of the animal, its realisation of its own nature and being, its awareness and control of environment, and the tasks needed to secure a living in and from that environment. This kind of rehearsal or dramatic play, in which the animal imitates various actions and becomes " other " animals—at one time the tracker, at another the pursued—at will, fully aware that this is not actuality (for it sheathes its claws and refrains its teeth from biting, however it puts on the mask of utter ferocity), is found with many of the higher animals.

2. *Drama and mankind*

Basically, this is drama. It is even ritual—a pattern begins to emerge in the play of the kittens, for certain actions are repeated, certain general approaches are used. Drama develops among human beings in a similar way—although man's relationships are, as soon as one can call him man, so much more subtle and complicated; but it involves the same impulse—to prepare himself for, to enter into satisfactory relationship with, his environment, to fulfil the nature of his being. This urges him on; and because he has higher intellectual powers, because he is so much more aware of, and able to analyse, his experience, the material of the dramatic process (which some of us see as the means and material of all his subsequent higher life) is much more varied though in essence the same. Man is conscious of, develops a response to, all forces and powers around him. These, no less than the simpler skills of physical action, are to be approached, in his drama; they are Gods, the Life Force, sometimes Saviours, sometimes enemies—

> As flies to wanton boys are we to the gods :
> They kill us for their sport,

says Gloucester in *King Lear*; while the King, in Kalidasa's *Sakuntala*, a thousand years earlier, laments in rather more philosophical terms that

> Every flower-tipt shaft
> Of Karma, as it probes our throbbing hearts,
> Seems to be barbed with hardest adamant.

Later, in each of these plays, the conflict with " the nature of things ", the " spiritual " environment, is resolved. This is not always the case—for drama presents men's continuing struggle, not his inevitable triumph and peace.

3.　*The earliest drama*

In the earliest dramatic performances known to us, the analogy with the " play " of the higher animals can be recognised. But man is reaching out, however uncertainly, further and further into the as yet unknown, bracing his mind for future adventure. His prime need was survival—and the food needed to ensure this. Whatever his natural sustenance, man, when he emerges into what we may regard as organised human life, in which purposive relations with environment are possible, is a hunter. Maybe he was forced into this by the needs of self-defence, adding to his strength and adaptability by the use of stones, later roughly shaped and chipped, to drive off the fierce animals who would prey on him. To use those he had killed for food, especially in changing conditions of climate, the hardships of the ice age or scarcity of vegetation, would be almost inevitable. From defence man passed to attack.

His pre-occupation with the powers of the animal world, his desire to acquire their strength, to combat them, to find power to live in control of the forces around him, may be seen in the earliest remains of communal life known to us—the paintings on the walls of the caves which he used, partly as shelter, but more probably for religious rites and tribal gathering.

Annette Laming tells us in *Lascaux: Paintings and Engravings* (Pelican Books) that the " first example of Palaeolithic art—an engraving of hinds on a fragment of bone " was discovered in the cave of Chaffaud in 1834. It was in 1879 that the little daughter of Don Marcelino S. de Sautuola (who was exploring the caves at Altamira) called out to her father that she could see some " bulls on the ceiling ". Looking up, he saw that there were painted and engraved animals in apparently wild confusion on the vault of the cave roof. The subsequent exploration and discussion of these paintings can be studied in Annette Laming's book—as well as many intricate problems that arise. For our purpose, whatever the total significance of the works of art, it may be enough to follow L. Adam in *Primitive Art* (Pelican Books) where he notes that many of the figures represent man as a hunter, the stalkers, weapons, and quarry. But—this is the significant fact—it is not the actual hunt that is depicted, even though actual animals are shown elsewhere in profusion. Where man enters, the painting is of a " pretended " hunt. Men are wearing masks and skins, while others encircle them. Here is a presentation of an actual "hunting mime" or drama, one which, before the cave artists came to their work, was an established and well organised ceremony. What they were attempting to do (physically) was to transfer this performance onto the walls of the cave, to perpetuate it, in this way, for whatever reason.

4. *The place and function of early drama*

We are told by the scholars skilled in such matters that primitive man tried by the hunting mime to establish a pattern; that pattern he believed would repeat itself in actuality. They give this the name of "sympathetic magic"; unfortunately, this may give the reader a rather condescending attitude to their efforts, for people do not believe in "magic" today. Luckily for the continuance of the human race no-one then told them that "magic" was an illusion—and they kept on with their careful rehearsal and patternmaking, believing that they could impose the pattern on their environment, and so secure in reality (as in pretended hunt) the animal they sought. The more knowledgeable sociologists of today tell us that man's achievement is largely through pattern making, in which, by voluntary organisation and discipline, he finds a way to realise himself in communal effort and thought. Such "patterns" will (if true) find a response in the environment to which they are "keyed". What the kittens did instinctively, men did with some thought. Maybe their thoughts were simply (to some extent) a justification of what they did instinctively; but they rehearsed, they learned the right movements, and—perhaps more important—they secured the right emotional preparation and communal "feeling" to go about a successful hunt. Drama uses the raw material of human experience, shaping it, re-arranging it, to explore further, and to secure the human being's happier relationship with life in the broad sense, including his own adjustment to the facts of existence, his co-operation with his fellows in social activity and culture, and his acceptance of all the powers which surround him—wind and rain, vegetable and animal creation, stars, sun, and moon, and those less tangible forces and powers which we all discuss and question at some time or another, the Gods.

Having secured a working pattern through the hunting mime, man sought to keep the pattern thus created in safety within the caves. He painted the hunting mime on their walls. From then on, artistically, many other factors intrude. We may note how man sought, was obsessed by, powers of life external, apparently, to himself, and tried to join himself with them, to acquire the animal's procreative force, the fertility and life of the forest, the wisdom and subtlety of the serpent. Further, we may see how for him all things " external " to himself were part of a living whole; the wind, the rain, the spring, the mountain, and the thunder, were alive in some way just as he was alive. Through the universe life manifested itself in infinite variety. Life could flow from one part to another, and could be encouraged to do so. The student should here refer to Jane Harrison's *Ancient Art and Ritual,* and to works on comparative religion such as A. C. Bouquet's volume in Penguin Books.

5. *From drama into ritual*

But the simple imitation of real action (while knowing full well that it is *not* real action) which we call mimesis, and which is the basis of drama, necessarily developed into a more organised and complex form as the size of the community grew, and its social organisation again (necessarily) more stringent and complex. Behind it now lay millenia of tradition and age-old wisdom which had to be preserved. At first, in the tiny groups of Palaeolithic times, all males might take part in the drama, while women stood round and (in time, one would think) added their cries of encouragement—the first " chorus " in the theatrical sense. From mimesis grew mime—certain recognised ways of imitating action which had been found acceptable, and became gradually stylised and symbolic. Skins and masks were worn from (one would judge) the dim beginnings, so as to ensure the possession of the animal's power and characteristics by the actor " impersonating " the quarry. Next, as the community grew, only the potential hunters would " act "; or (a contrary tendency) on some occasions chosen leaders, those wise in tradition and the effective performance of " magic ", might do much of the presentation.

Study of existing rituals shows the great variety possible from a common origin and identical basis. Further, the need to control and to co-ordinate larger numbers of actors, and the demand that the *correct* actions be achieved, would lead to a more stylised and ritualistic performance. The resulting rhythmic pattern of movement might be accompanied by the clapping of hands, the encouraging (but wordless) shouting or wailing (note how many early dances and rituals have apparently meaningless vocal accompaniment—musical rather than linguistic) and the development of the first musical instruments, percussion, drum,

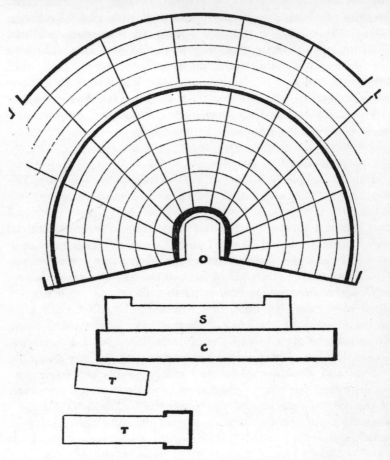

Fig. 1.—Sketch plan of the Temple of Dionysos at Athens.
T—temple.   S—stage.   O—orchestra

cymbals, gong; the subsequent elaboration may be imagined, or indeed witnessed today as part of a great communal religious gathering in the uplands of Nepal or the Tibetan borders.

6.   *The dramas of life and resurrection*

As man changed from a hunting animal into a pastoralist and (more significantly) into a farmer, so his dramatic activities also

changed. Now he does not mime the successful hunt, or re-tell
the story of some demi-god's success in the field, so as to make
that success his own, or to inspire emulation amongst the
younger; instead, he shows, in mimesis at first, and later with
developing pattern and ritual the sowing of the seed and the
reaping of the harvest, as did the Indonesian dancers who visited
our country in the fifties; here, vividly the whole process of seed-
time and harvest moved before us. The burial of the seed, the
growth, the resurrection from the ground, the movement of the
seasons—these are now the rhythms to which man moves. When
he was a hunter he was conscious of changing climate and
weather; but now that he relies on the fertility of the field, there
comes the more terrifying "death" of mid-winter. Life must
then be renewed—so that he may be renewed with it. So we
have all the mid-winter dramas and festivals, of which our own

Fig. 2.—Kandyan dance: associated at first with Hindu religious
practice, and now with Buddhism.

Yule and its associated plays (e.g. *St. George and the Dragon*) are survivals. Further, now that he is forced into a closer relationship with the movements of the earth, the stars, and the sun, and feels anew his dependence on, his essential harmony (ideally) with, the life forces, his mind reaches out again to the powers behind—the Life Force itself, however conceived, whether Dionysos, Tammuz, the dying year, the resurrection life, " the purple self-existent god whose vital energy pervades all space " (from the Sanskrit : Bharata's treatise on drama, 3rd century A.D.), the ultimate questions of his own being and fate. All these things constitute for him his larger environment, and are now largely independent of that control over material things which was his first dramatic quest, or even the harnessing of the forces of nature, the colonisation of distant lands or the planets themselves ! These comprehensive problems occupy his attention and are explored through his drama.

7. *Drama and Liturgy*

From the start drama was associated, as we have seen, with man's total response to his environment, a response which involves " religion ". One important development, which, as we shall see, occurs all over the world, is the further stylising of dramatic " rituals " into " liturgy "—in other words a corporate act of worship involving the Powers which govern man's life and activities, the Ultimate Environment. This " liturgy "—the word means " public (or communal) work and service " and the termination is related to our word " urge " or " energy "—is the active approach of the society to the sources of its life and being. No longer is man concerned merely to secure the flesh of the wild animal through " sympathy " and association with the powers that be; now he seeks the Life Force, the creative fertility of Dionysos, or the spiritual Body and Blood of Immanent and Transcendent Deity. (Students should note that we are here stating facts relevant to the study of drama. From the sociological or religious angle there is very much more to be said.) Normally, it is from an ordered liturgy that theatre derives. In other words, (1) dramatic activity becomes ritual, (2) the ritual becomes liturgy, with the separation (already started in an earlier stage) of celebrants, actors in the Divine Mystery, from the congregation of worshippers (who, however, even as audience actively participate through response and action, either individually, or through representatives), and then (3) the liturgy becomes the theatrical performance. The priests gradually withdraw as details of the liturgy become more and more developed. We are familiar with this process in Greece, where religious worship involved recounting the deeds of the God and those events associated with him (and including humans) gradually widened to allow stories of the Gods in general and the great and eternal questions of Life, Death, and Fate, to be presented.

We are familiar, too, with the same process in mediaeval drama, when, from the Mass, first " tropes " and then complete plays developed. Yet theatre rarely, if ever, moves completely from its basis in religion and ritual. In Malaya, the priest accompanies the touring Ma-yong company; the Chinese opera players solemnly cense the stage before the performance in their London presentations; and even the most naturalistic and materialistic modern drama manifests—to the alert mind—some of those religious and ritual elements (in the broad sense) which are part of theatre art and the dramatic approach to the content of life.

8. *The content of theatre*

The elements in drama and theatre which we have summarised so far will be found in endless variety and differing combinations in the cultures of the world. Theatre is a complex form involving many apparently independent arts which have grown up under its encouragement and as part of its own life. Often, the primitive mime, with its added rhythmic music, will emphasise, and develop into, dance; indeed this is the origin of dance proper. Sometimes, chanted words accompany the action, or tell the story—and we gradually evolve the spoken dialogue characteristic of the Greek and Roman drama, classical Indian, or the modern Western Theatre. On the other hand, the Javanese often preserve these elements in equal proportion, both dance and spoken dialogue. From the start we have seen the use of masks and disguises—" costume " in modern phrase—often with other involved make-up, which conveys important information to the audience. We have noted that drama spans the whole of experience, from the simple need to find food to the unending search for what Shakespeare called " the mystery of things " —from the mud to the very Heaven of Heavens.

Finally, we must be prepared to find theatre in which all these elements are combined. Such is the Chinese, with ritual, sym-

bolism, percussion accompaniment, stylised diction, dance, intricate mime, animal disguises, and sheer acrobatics, all united in a
total and wholly satisfying " performance ", with variety of
musical instruments and " operatic " conventions. This " total "

FIG. 3.—Hellmouth in a Western mediaeval religious play.

theatre is now influencing Western presentation; stylising,
symbolism, and the abandonment of " straight " dialogue as the
means of communication, are noticed in the work of our own
playwrights; and on the other hand, music is returning (not
merely as " melodrama " accompaniment in television or film)
but also as an integral part of dramatic presentation; the new
musical play, neither a straight naturalistic play, nor a musical
comedy, nor a comedy with music, is a theatre form in itself,
uniting dance, song, and dialogue, a serious and important

development in Western theatre. Apart from general influence and trend, we have the direct interplay in décor, costume, and theme, of east and west from plays of Yeats inspired by Japanese Nō drama, and the expressionist productions of the twenties, to the Brechtian drama of the forties and fifties, such a presentation, for example, as *The Caucasian Chalk Circle*.

All that we have discussed above may be seen in the mimes, dances, dance drama, rituals and dramatic performances of peoples and tribes at the present time, or as recorded by sociologists and qualified observers in written records of the last century.

CHAPTER II

THE BACKGROUND OF DRAMA

All over the world, in every tribe and people, there are rituals which bring humanity into profitable relationship with environment, establish rhythms of custom and behaviour, and pattern the life attitudes, providing a dynamic and a way to communal fulfilment. These rituals begin as mimesis, and move on into dance and/or drama. Primitive tribes still existing today provide us with examples of stages in the evolution of drama and its progress into theatre. We may take material almost at random from various parts of the world.

1. *Mimetic actions and the struggle for life*

War dances may be performed by women to help absent husbands who are fighting. Among Tshi peoples on the Gold Coast, wives painted themselves white, and on the day of the combat ran about armed with guns or sticks shaped to represent guns, then took green paw-paws (a fruit shaped like a melon) and cut these with knives as if taking the head of an enemy. In British Columbia women in similar circumstances danced, performing a mime of attack and defence, throwing hooked sticks forward in aggression or drawing the hooked end back as if taking a man out of danger. Weapons were always pointed towards the enemy country. Faces were painted red, and accompanying songs prayed that the weapons might help their husbands.

Mimetic actions to secure rain are found the world over. Formerly in Russia, near Dorpat, three men used to climb a fir tree in a sacred grove. One hit a kettle or cask to produce the rattle of thunder; another swung fire-brands together, the resultant sparks simulating lightning; and the third, the actual rain maker, sprinkled water around from a bundle of twigs. Similar mimetic methods of stopping rain were used. Medicine men at Port Stephens in New South Wales threw firebrands in the air, shouting and puffing to blow away the clouds at the same time.

Survivals of tree worship, connected with the promotion of fertility, are obvious enough throughout civilised Europe, and the resultant rituals and semi-dramatic actions are wide-spread. On the Thursday before Whit Sunday Russian villagers used to go to the woods, sing, weave garlands, and secure a young birch tree, which was dressed in women's clothes. The dressed-up tree was carried back to the village again with songs. The tree was left in a house, and visited as a guest until Whit Sunday. On Whit Sunday, the tree was taken to a stream and thrown in, the garlands being thrown after her. The spirit of growth was personified, and the tree (or woman) finally married with the life-giving water, probably a rain charm.

Swedish ceremonies, particularly at Midsummer, are well known. The raising of the maypole was an important occasion; it seemed to represent the male principle, the girls lugging it up into position. And, of course, our own writers tell of such ceremonies: " Against May, Whitsonday, or some other time, all the yung men and wives, run gadding over night to the woods, groves, hills, and mountains. . . . The chiefest jewel they bring from thence is their May-pole, which they bring home with great veneration, as thus: They have twentie or fortie yoke of oxen every oxe having a sweet nose gay of floures placed on the tip of his hornes and these oxen drawe home this May-pole (this stinkying ydol, rather) that is covered all over with floures and hearbes, bound round with stringes, from the top to the bottome, and sometimes painted with variable colours, with two or three hundred men, women and children following it with great devotion . . . And then fall they to daunce about it like as the heathen people did at the dedication of the Idols, whereof this is a perfect pattern or rather the thing itself."

But this attenuated rite (surviving in a Christian country though in essence, as Stubbs stated in the above words, from an early religion) hardly shows specific dramatic intent, however this actually inspired the original dance and worship. Let us look at old customs in Bohemia, where not merely dance, but dialogue, action, and puppetry enter, to present dramatically the death of the old and the birth of the new life. On the fourth

Sunday in Lent a puppet called Death was thrown into water; then girls went to the woods, cut down a young tree, fastening to it a puppet dressed as a woman in white clothes. This doll, personifying the spirit life of the tree, is then carried from house to house, while they sing, the refrain being

> We carry death out of the village,
> We bring Summer into the village.

So we come to the Green George ceremonies, still known in parts of Britain and the Continent, often associated with the actual Mumming Plays.

All over the world such rites are found. As Frazer points out, the contrast between dormant vegetation in Winter and the active life of the Summer is represented by " a dramatic contest between actors who play the parts respectively of Winter and Summer ". In his day this was still (for the Esquimaux of Central North America) actually magical in power. The Esquimaux divided into two parties, the ptarmigan and the ducks, the former all those born in winter, the latter those in summer. Then ensued a tug of war with a long sealskin rope. All hoped that the ptarmigans would lose—for then summer won and fine weather would be the rule.

Similarly, in more developed dramatic form, at Dromling in Brunswick the contest is presented by a troupe of boys and a troupe of girls. The boys shout and ring bells to drive winter away as they go from house to house; the girls follow singing, led by a May Bride, in gay dresses to present the flowery colours and warmth of Spring. Winter was formerly carried in the form of a straw puppet by the boys; when Frazer wrote it was acted by a real man.

2.   *The dramatised struggle and its conventions*

The evolution of drama in a community whose round of seasonal work, festivity, and social activity, depends on, and is harmonised by, religion was seen in the film *Sherpa* (with a commentary by David Attenborough). Here, on the borders of Nepal and Tibet, the same Buddhism which so largely inspired the development of drama in China and Japan, governs the worship, entertainment, and daily actions of the people. In a great festival at the Buddist monastery the monks perform, after careful rehearsal, the temple dance which inaugurates the full ritual, designed to ensure safety and fertility for the crops, and to drive far away the forces of evil, powerful to destroy the food of the population, but representing, too, the things that harm and obliterate the higher life of man. The " audience " has already developed from the " congregation " for although they are vitally concerned with the correct performance of the ritual, which will affect their own lives, they stand, sit, and gaze as the careful performers achieve every action.

In a white mask, presenting advanced years, the spirit of aged and doddering wisdom, comes a " lama " (in character); the audience laugh at his uncertainty—but not unkindly; here is the genesis of stage humour. Then the black-hatted magicians dance and are worsted—for they present the old gods of the country, driven out by successful Buddhism—a little dramatised history; there are jesters, who entertain the souls of the happy—it is interesting to see how the basically religious act of worship logically introduces entertainment and fun; enter the skull faced demons who play out their warfare against man—represented in this episode by a puppet. Thus the demons are driven out from the valley by sympathetic magic. As the dance triumphs, so will they be unable in actual fact to do evil. The audience (or worshippers and sharers in the ritual, and after all an audience is always both these things) achieve the triumph with the actors; so happiness and prosperity come to the valley. The old struggle between good and evil, life and no-life, creation and destruction, is played out in this superb mystery drama, with its grotesque masks and its sense of urgency. Here is the whole range of drama, tragedy, comedy, farce, and variety show. (Most impressive was the mask of a chief God. His terrifying aspect, however, was to drive away the demons. To humanity he was kind.)

Such rituals and dramatic enactments exist over the world. In more cultured communities they appear as folk plays and popular customs, surviving as such with the later religion (often superimposed) and a mature theatrical tradition. Sometimes they have vanished, because incorporated into the theatre of the country. Where, however, a new religion and culture has been brought from outside, they are often tolerated as old customs. It is, therefore, rare to find them in vitality and full expression; either they have developed further, or they have been suppressed and weakened. Few tribes exist where dramatic and mimetic practices exist today in their primitive significance; and anthropologists are trying to record such activities wherever they can find them unimpaired. They still thrive in simple communities which are (at the same time) sufficiently developed culturally. In the Himalayas, where the rural community has survived for a long time without outside intrusion, it is able to perpetuate with sincerity and energy the dramatic presentations needed to ensure fertility and to drive away destructive forces.

But glance at any part of *The Golden Bough,* and you will see the universality of similar approaches designed to secure the life forces : worship of trees among the Warika of East Africa, the fire ceremonies of the Berbers, the death and resurrection enactments of Ceram, or in North America masked dances, whatever their particular significance. Among the Indians of Nootka Sound there is a ritual death and a rebirth by means of persons who are dressed and masked as wolves, or other " totem " animal. Here there is the desire to enlist the spirit of an animal (as part of the mighty life force) in the service of man, a specialisation of the more general idea of entering into fruitful relationship with one's environment. The sacrifice of the " divine animal " who possesses the energy and life (which the tribe desire to share) has been recorded in detail from travellers' accounts of these ceremonies among the Gilyaks of Siberia. Here magical practices are mingled with symbolic presentation and dance involving the whole community—with a long address to a captive bear who seems to the tribe to contain the desired vital powers. In one district the bear was admonished to do his duty, to tell the gods to bring riches, to make sure hunters return laden with furs and flesh. In brief, the bear becomes a minor deity, and is addressed as such. For the student of drama interest lies in the rituals and mass enactments which group round the attempt to share the full life of the creation, and, further, in the relevance of these enactments to the animal disguises which figure so largely in drama, in children's, or in fantasy, plays (even sourly and satirically, as in *The Insect Play*) at the present time.

Perhaps the most eloquent assessment of primitive feeling for the new life, the seasonal manifestation of the powers by which we live, is given by Fraser in his description, under the heading of " The Magic Spring ", of the transformation of desert in Central Australia, aided (so the aborigines thought) by appropriate rites to encourage the rebirth of nature. He paints a striking picture of the barren land suddenly bursting into vegetation and teeming animal activity; and he notes that such an outburst before a favourable season seems to be anticipated by an extra celebration of the " magical " rituals. But—and this is for us important—these " spring " rituals " bear a close analogy " to surviving customs of European peasantry. Humanity and the dramatic process are one round the world.

3. Survivals of early drama as acted today

In Europe we have an opportunity to study the development (and the survival in almost meaningless forms) of primitive dramatic presentations. On the one side we have the movement from Greek rituals into full theatre; on the other the survival in Greece (possibly till today, certainly to late Victorian times) of a broken remnant of the same Dionysiac fertility cult. In this two men, dressed in goat skins and masks, accompanied by two boys dressed as brides, parade the village, accompanied by an " old woman carrying a child of unknown birth ". The men carry a cross bow and a wooden phallic emblem. The events of the somewhat lengthy play, the fight against winter, the acceptance of the new life (the baby), the mock marriage, and the final yoking of the boys to the plough which shall ensure the food supply, unite to typify the creative force that is enlisted.

Here is a folk remembrance of Dionysiac dramatic rituals, which the various emblems typify. Equally, in even more primitive dances which have come down to us, the imitation of rain, clouds, winds, shows the derivation from an early mimesis in which the forces by which man was surrounded were made, in essence, his own. As Dr. James has pointed out, the more primitive the dance, the greater the element of mimesis; as in visual art, stylising comes later. We are on safe ground when we teach children to move and to enter on their dramatic heritage through such mimesis, movement motivated dramatically by the urge to do and to be, not movement for the sake of movement.

Some examples of such dance and mimetic survival in our own country may be studied.

In North Lincoln the struggle for the Haxey Hood persists. A procession, headed by the Fool, accompanies the twelve Boggans, or players; the Fool after the ringing of the church bells, proclaims the struggle, with a reference to two bullocks and a half —the fight is to be for the other " half bullock ", now represented

c

by the similarly shaped hood. After some preliminary skirmishes for less important " hoods ", the real object is thrown in. The aim is to prevent any outsiders from securing it. The struggling pack of men surge one way and the other in this "winter solstice " game. (The actual date is sufficiently near for this to be a typical " turn of the year " festival, a fight which warms up not only the contestants, but the whole community and the sleeping forces of nature.) The effort to win the flesh which embodies the bull life guarantees renewed fertility in the New Year and accords with similar ritual struggles and dramas in other places.

A spring time dance drama in which we use rites which, by their rhythmic quality, shall stimulate the growing powers of the earth is found in the Morris dances, for example, of Bampton in Oxfordshire. The " Green Man " who occurs in country processions and ceremonies is an annual victim in the vegetation dramas, surrendering his life, the vital sap in plants and trees, to revive earth to renewed effort. The " Jack-in-the-Green " which used to parade the streets of London had something of the same magic power. But in some stories and observances the Green Man becomes an almost terrifying nature spirit, instinct with awful power, an elemental force.

Here, we should note, we meet another strange quality of dramatic ritual; an original myth (attached to a particular ritual) attracts to itself all kinds of other material—stories and legends —and groups these round its central theme or urge. Thus to the spring time " Green Man " were assimilated stories about Robin Hood—who had some slight reality once as a historical figure, but who now becomes a kind of cult hero. We have fragments of folk plays dealing with him and his men, while Maid Marion, as the female principle in creation, intrudes from many older rites. And so we have our first real native plays. But note how this original basis has maintained its place; Robin Hood has helped popular television drama considerably. He struts the pantomime stage, he figures in many plays made for children; to him there still belongs the allure which surrounds a fundamental human response to life.

In Greece, similarly, to the worship of Dionysos were added different stories of men and gods to diversify the original observance in honour of the god of new life and fertility. To the early tropes on the Easter story were soon attached all kinds of events,

Biblical and non-Biblical, to be a foundation of modern western theatre. But under all lies the basic impulse : to secure and align oneself with the life forces, the essentials of being.

For a play within our own tradition which originates from winter festivals to secure new life and ensure resurrection, we can instance the St. George and the Dragon mummers' play found in so many versions in England. Here, indeed, are most of the elements of drama, the transformation into characters of forces originally invoked, taking to themselves the names and stories of new figures; St. George enters the play with his Christian associations, and the farcical dialogue of the doctor utilises immediate audience response. The gusto with which modern " educated " audiences and actors enjoy and present this play witnesses to some age-long potency of appeal, as does its excellence as a training piece for younger actors. Here is the embryonic Dionysos, the dramatic egg; children and actors to-day accept it simply as a traditional piece of nonsensical play. But they experience in it most of the dramatic situations and emotional patterns which later they will refine and utilise in more developed and complex art forms of theatre. For here are also the ritual combat, the struggle to ensure new life at the Winter Solstice, the death and resurrection enactment, lamentation followed by mirth and thank-offering.

Ceylon exhibits in existing dance and drama (probably as well as any other country) various levels of development from earliest times. Here are still performed the native Sinhalese devil dances to exorcise sickness from ailing persons. A shrine is erected, with a dais for the sick person, and the ceremonies commence in the evening. Drummers and singers accompany the mimetic dance to persuade away the demons who have attacked the victim; men dancers dress as women to attract the demons to themselves. Then, after the night has passed in a continuous ritual, about four a.m. the dancers put on masks. They themselves are now the demons, announce their new " character " as they run round, and (possessed by the evil spirits) reveal the motives which led to the attack on the sick person. Here is ritual, sympathetic magic, impersonation, the elaborately built shrine or " theatre " house with walls of plaited stems and palm leaves, dance and drama of fantastic costumes and masks.

In Ceylon there is preserved also a careful tradition of sophisticated and artistic dance, introduced from India by Buddhist missionaries two thousand years ago. Under the patronage of the Kandyan kings from the sixteenth to nineteenth centuries, it is now encouraged in the High Schools and assisted by the temples, still forming an important element in religious festivals, such as the Procession at the Showing of Buddha's Tooth. Founded on symbolic action relevant to Rathna and Ganesa, it has added other themes from mythology and court life. The costumes of beaten silver, the wide plaques and heavy bracelets, are familiar to us from travel books. Men only take part, the gestures and hand movements being basically those of Indian dance. The dramatic element has become obscured in the dancer's art.

However, other drama is linked with the devil dancing. Comedy skits relevant to everyday life are inserted to relieve the strain of the lengthy ritual. Folk-lore tales, improvisation, or a ready made repertory of playlets, are used at will by the troupes.

But the full emergence of folk drama is seen in Kolam, a word meaning " guise " or " representation ". Here, to the accompaniment of drummers and musicians, the story is told simply. The

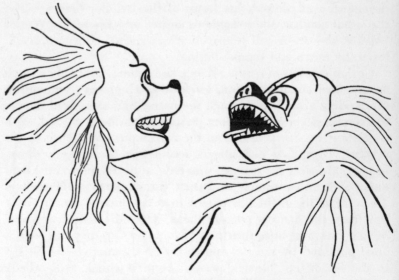

Fig. 4.—Animal masks in a Kolam folk play (Ceylon).

masked characters enter in succession to dance briefly. Speeches in the actual play are short—for the royal characters can hardly move under the weight of imposing masks and can remain before the audience only for a short time. The cast includes demons, a lion, jackals, and the fabulous " kinnaras ", half human, half bird. Buddha prevents an unhappy climax, when he saves the " kinnaras " from destruction at the king's hand. The events take place in India. Here are the genuine elements of folk drama emerging from a religious and ritual background—supernaturals, animal characters, fairy story, dance, music, and dialogue.

Note a final " layer " of dramatic activity developing in Ceylon *ab initio* from the ritual of another faith—the Sinhalese (Christian) passion play. Narrative and chorus accompany the procession of statues representing Christ Mary, and Joseph. At one time (this is now forbidden) women impersonated our Lady. Just as in the serious " devil " dance, comedy evolves alongside the " tragedy ", only here it is the " devils " (led by Lucifer) who furnish the fun. Village boys run round, impersonating the evil spirits, and declaiming local scandal and gossip—the embryonic Aristophanic impulse These plays are now under careful control and stricter regulation !

4. *Survivals of early drama—children's traditional games*

Fig. 5.—Western " mummers " from Cotton. manuscript.
(Adapted from Knight's *Old England*.)

Yet the early dramas survive (in lively fashion) best of all among children. Here the theories of the scholar have little place; these *are* the dramas themselves. And so long as children are allowed to *grow* up (we are doing our best in many ways to prevent the process, denying them the playing space and conditions in which they can, through childhood enjoyed, really develop as people) and are not *forced* up to become neurotic immature adults—so long these games and rituals will persist. A film, *One Potato, Two Potato,* shot in the streets of London, recorded for all time some of these games—the properly dramatic " ring " and " arch " games, the incantation and ritual games, and the hunting and chasing mimes of struggle. Decayed from original fullness, they still exhibit adequately the genesis of drama.

If the arts are to survive, " imagination ", creativity, aesthetic sense and achievement, to persist, and human beings to remain human, not, dominated by the machines they have made, to become less than their own manufactures, children need to explore and develop through such experiences, to attain a real maturity.

Watch one of the games—the ring of children, the princess in the middle, the entry of the witch, the dying princess on the ground, the circle which, dancing clockwise, invokes the powers of life. Now the prince breaks the ring and revives the princess. Here is dance, ritual and drama, death and resurrection, tragedy (man in opposition to the forces of death he must meet, the hardness of creation), comedy, the happy union of the prince and princess for renewed life, and the chanting magic circle. Always *improvisation* as a fresh child undertakes the part, and always a *permanent* dramatic pattern as the basic actions are repeated.

CHAPTER III

THE FIRST PLAYS AND THE COMING OF THE "ACTOR"

Mimesis becomes mime; mime becomes pattern; mime stylised becomes dance; dance becomes ritual; ritual is enshrined in liturgy. (This simple statement may be elaborated by what follows.)

Liturgy, then, becomes drama when those taking part, in addition to their official status, impersonate characters other than their own. In a sense drama is inherent both in the origin of liturgy and also in the fact that a priest is performing certain actions as a "representative"—sometimes of *people*, sometimes of a *ruler*, sometimes of the *God*. But the significant development arises when more expanded myth is added to the liturgy and story and plot are established. Much has been written on the nature and origin of "myth"; whatever view is taken, however, the "myth" exhibits, in the guise of a story, some of the fundamental experiences of mankind. Typically, it portrays, under the statement of actual events, the seasonal cycle, the death of winter and the resurrection of spring, the combat of life against death, of light against darkness, features reproduced, often with historic figures, in more developed theatre (cp. *Macbeth*), for the simple reason that our own lives (as individuals) are constantly involved in these struggles. A myth is the reverse of a falsity; it is a symbol of the living pattern of our world, a channel into which we can constantly direct our own thoughts and experience.

1. *Ancient Egypt*

Perhaps the oldest written drama known is the Coronation Play of ancient Egypt; a text exists from the time of Sesotris I

39

Fig. 6.—A Bugaku masked actor in a primitive Indian
dance drama surviving only in Japan, where it came,
as also to China, through Buddhist influence. This art is
preserved only at the Imperial Court and at certain
shrines.

(c. 1970 B.C.). It is, however, sometimes regarded by competent
scholars as dating from the time of the first dynasty (c. 3300
B.C.). It demonstrates the two aspects of *kenosis* (emptying, by

purification and preparation) and *plerosis* (the filling with new
life) which characterise seasonal mimetic rituals. Such aspects
naturally are reflected in developed theatre. The exposition
(kenosis) sets matters in a state of preparedness, clears away
other thoughts from minds of the audience, and orders everything for the reception *(plerosis)* of the new life experience.
(Kenosis may be illustrated in Christian liturgy by the
" asperges " at the start of Mass; *plerosis* by the imparting of the
full life of Christ to the believer is the work of later parts of the
ceremonial.)

Gaster, in his great work *Thespis,* has analysed this primitive drama into typical components, deriving from various
aspects of earlier myth and ritual. So he groups its forty-six
scenes to show the basic pattern. (We should note that among
some tribes the old king must be killed when he fails in vitality,
for the health of the tribe is bound up in him, their representative. In his place reigns the virile heir. In time the Egyptians
came to substitute a symbolic renewal for such direct action. The
old king attains, and rises to new life by association with the
life of the God.) Fertility rites are performed in scenes 5, 9, 19,
the burial of the old king and resurrection as a new king, in
scenes 3, 13-15, 26-28, the ritual combat in scene 18, the equipment of the royal barge to tour royal cities, sharing the kingly
life and power, in scenes 1, 2, 7, 10-11 and 16. The new king is
invested and installed in scenes 6, 8, 23-25, 27-28, 31,
33, 35. The communal feast to which the governors of the
various "nomes" are invited occupies scenes 21-22, 30, 32,
43-44. Each actor represents other people, as in a full drama.
Thus two priestesses who perform the wailing for the departure
of the earth's warmth and growth, the " seasonal ululation " as
Gaster terms it (cp. the wailing for Tammuz in the Middle
East) represent also Isis and Nepthys bewailing Osiris, slain in
the mythic story. Puns are used to point mythic symbolism. So
Set thrashes his father Osiris—and the word for " grain " is
similar to that for " father ". The function of Osiris as a god of
life and fertility, resurrected in the living grain, is indicated.

In fact, every original ritual act is now explained in terms of
the myth. Dialogue and speakers are used again to symbolise the
" plot ". So there are at this stage three levels of interpretation,
(1) the ritual itself, (2) the dramatic presentation which emerges
from this, and (3) the mythic significance which completes the

circle back to the first—for the performers of the ritual are also the actors in the mythic story.

In scene 30, for example, the ritual involves the ceremonial invitation of the governors of various districts. But, adds a note, here the " actors " are really showing the invitation of the gods by Thoth to attend on Horus. Then follows the simple dialogue. Thoth says :

> Come, wait upon the presence of Horus.
> Thou, Horus, art their lord.

Stage directions indicate the arrival of the governors, again with the note that they represent the attendance of the gods on Horus. The student may find that development of drama from Christian liturgy will still further indicate the process. Here clergy, acting a ritual, at the same time come to represent people in the Resurrection story in very much the same way. Similarly, at Epiphany the three ministers at Mass impersonated also (at twelfth century Rouen) the three Magi. So we find the origin of the " actor " in the more specialised sense of this word.

2. *Plays from the Middle East*

Ancient Hittite drama even has its own named writer, the priest Kellas, who wrote the " Puruli play " about 1350 B.C. Here we have a fascinating blend, the evolving forms of theatre demonstrated. First comes a recital and invocation to ensure fertility. Then follows the enactment of the myth—the dragon overcome by the weather god, the seasonal strife. (Compare the killing of the dragon by St. George in the Christianised British Mummers Play enacted at the Winter Solstice.) The last part of the play presents ritual concerned with the divine images. Again, the preparation, the " agon ", and the plerosis, the filling of life with the God-like influence.

Most interesting is the Canaanite Ras Shamra play, the poem of " Dawn and Sunset ". Here we come even closer to the drama of ancient Greece. After an introductory intercession and address to the audience of votaries, the vinedressers enter to prune and lop the vines, an operation which they represent as the suffering of Dionysos (to use a more familiar name for the god). This ritual is repeated seven times. Statues of the gods are then brought in, and a hymn ends the ritual introduction. (This

ritual became in time the " prologue " to a regular drama. See
Gaster, op. cit., p. 248.) The actual play follows. The aged El
is seen standing by his house. He fetches water and shoots a
bird. Two women standing by are attracted by his vigour and
ability. Coyly, they offer themselves either as daughters or as
wives. El accepts them as his wives. Two Divine children are
born—Dawn and Sunset. (Needless to say this is reported to El
by a messenger.) Now comes the first intermission—in the form
of an offering of gifts to the Lady Sun and the fixed stars. We
now return to the two Divine children; their prowess (in appetite
and strength) is narrated by the human husband of the two
women. At a second intermission further offerings are made.
The next " act "—to use the later term—shows the children
roaming over the earth, devouring the grain, demanding that
" custodians " open up the barns for them. Here, unfortunately,
the text ends. Sufficient has remained for scholars to see clearly
the pattern of this play, which can be expanded by reference to
other rituals. Here is the sacred marriage, which is featured in
many ceremonies linked with fertility. Here, too, are the divine
offspring, with gargantuan appetites, surviving even today in
Macedonian and Thracian folk-plays, presented at Carnival.

For many reasons, Gaster thinks that the play was designed
for the Canaanite festival of the first-fruits. He compares the
Israelite Feast of Weeks, or Pentecost. Dawn and Sunset may be
identified as the Heavenly Twins and in Babylonian and Jewish
Calendars the Twins are the regents of the month of June, the
time of this festival. An interesting suggestion is that we have
here a parallel with the ancient Laconian festival of Hyakinthia.
Hyakinthos (Wakuntas?) was an ancient Minoan vegetation god,
supplanted by Apollo after the Greek invasion. He was (like
Osiris and Adonis) lamented and mourned seasonally, such sor-
row being followed by rejoicing.

In this play we have, then, myth activating ritual into drama.
There is a pattern of prologue, episode, procession (or intermission) and song of adoration, episode, intermission, and so on.
The plot shows how the fruits of the earth are secured through
the aged but ever vigorous God, and depicts the annual birth
of powers that rule the season, governors of the long summer day.

3.   From liturgy to theatre in Greece

Let us glance briefly at the Greek theatre. In the *Bacchae* of

Euripides, it has been noted, the seasonal sequences are clothed in just sufficient myth to make a story. It contains all the elements of the basic ritual which produced the drama in Greece—timbrels, fawnskin, and ivy, the god emblematised as snake, bull, and lion, the dawn dance on the mountain, and the fertility symbols—old men rejuvenated, the beardless god, and the man disguised as a woman.

Studying the first choral ode, which directly indicates the worshipping community and their devotion, one may note that here we have a stylised and literary version of the original ritual chant. Here a whole process is exemplified—the first mimetic approach becomes the primitive ritual; the primitive ritual becomes the seasonal drama; this stylises to liturgical chant; and then from the liturgical chant re-emerges (as so often in classical Greek theatre) the full theatrical presentation.

But although the *Bacchae* obviously by its theme links closely with religious origins, the same dependence and pattern may be seen almost as plainly in other plays. We have noted the elements of the ritual plays; these elements emerge quite definitely in typical Greek tragedy. Euripidean drama plans round the sequence of agon (or combat), mourning (or pathos), lamentation (to bring back the lord of fertility) (threnos), and final epiphany. Euripides has been too often studied from the viewpoint of the twentieth century; we try to find in him our own attitudes; this is all very well so long as we ascribe to him the feelings of our common humanity, but when we try to read into his work our own peculiar contemporary approaches to life, we may be in danger of misunderstanding. Let us realise that there was another " side "—the centuries of accumulated worship and belief which preceded, underlay, and were accepted by the spectators of, his plays. On the other hand, we have here ever present and ever contemporary necessities of theatre—preparation, conflict, suffering, mourning, and resolution—the restoration of balance in some form or another, working out the conflicts in life.

4. *Liturgical drama and literature*

Literature itself originates in drama, generally from the liturgical and early theatrical forms. It is often easy to see this (e.g. in some Japanese texts the full writing of stage-directions, setting, and description of action, enables the play to be read as if it were a novel) but the matter goes deeper. We have noted the great choral odes of Greek tragedy, based on earlier rituals.

Fig. 7.—The masked king in a Kolam folk drama.

Let us recall an old Indian story. Mind and Speech came before God and asked Him to decide which was the greater. God answered that Mind was the greater; Speech but imitated its actions and walked in its footsteps.

Actually, literature owes much to theatre. Gaster has shown with some probability that many texts regarded as " literature " are in reality " frozen " dramas. We have noted above the ability of ritual to develop drama, which then swings back into ritual, as in the choral odes. In the literature of the Bible we have perhaps the same process. Psalm 68 may well be the libretto of a seasonal " pantomime " for the New Year (compare the Egyptian and Canaanite " pantomimes " above) arranged in literary form as a formal psalm to be used in the worship of Yahweh. Poetry, both ode and lyric, later prose, story, and narrative, all alike stem from drama. Drama has a valid sociological function; to quote the terms of a great scholar, its work here is, in all kinds of possible ways, to revive the " topocosm ", i.e., the entire complex of any region of our world conceived as living organism. In reviving, it also entertains. (A consideration of what real " entertainment " involves may make this clear to the student!) And from the revival come varied forms of human expression, literature not the least.

Chapter IV

CHINA

1. Historical background

It is appropriate to start our survey of more developed theatre
with China; for this great culture, or series of cultures, exhibits
widely and variously all that we understand by drama, showing
in its history the way from dance, ritual, and folk celebration, to
liturgy, performance, and then to professional theatre of differing
styles. Further, there is decay and revival, the intricate turning
back upon itself characteristic of theatre, renewal from the
sources; there is, too, the involved pattern of relationship with
the ruling authorities and general populace, one of the recurrent
difficulties of theatre and drama. The problem of theatrical survival is ever with us. But Chinese reverence for the past, for what
we may call human achievement and heritage, has ensured
through all a certain continuity and coherence.

The semi-nomadic peoples of China established during the
period 3000-2000 B.C. settled communities with the development
of agriculture in the valleys of the Yangtze-kiang and Hoang-ho;
China had its own civilisation parallel in time with that of the
Sumerians in Babylonia and the Old Kingdom in Egypt. Excavations have shown the use in the Shang dynasty (1766-
1122 B.C.) of simple percussion and flute, almost inevitably indicative of ceremonial and simple dance drama. The Shih Ching
(Book of Songs) dating, perhaps, from the end of this dynasty
collects together much of the vocal material used. At the turn
of the season, naturally in a community dependent on agriculture, a chorus of boys and another chorus of girls (from
different villages) met near places where rivers flowed together.
One choir answered another in short sequences, accompanied by

47

gesture. This antiphonal singing by the sexes dramatically symbolised the two principles of the universe Yang and Yin, which,
working in unity, bring harmony and fertility. So, too, the rivers
joined their power. Today, three thousand years later, we can
see on film the same separation of the sexes in answering chant
and song in the blessing of rice fields beneath Mount Fuyji in
Japan. Symbolism is born in such simple dramatic rites, but
becomes more and more subtle and important as time goes on,
until today it may be termed a major method of human communication in the arts.

From these early times originated the five note scale,
the basis of Chinese melody, especially associated with Mongoloid peoples (e.g. in America also) even if originally shared
throughout cultures of the New Stone and Bronze Ages. Similarly, music itself and its tones and notes have symbolic significance, a link with the fundamental harmony and essence of the
universe. (Cp. Plato's opinions.)

With the Chou dynasty (1050-255 B.C.) there appear many
other musical instruments. Some experts regard this period as
marking the highest achievements of Chinese civilisation (in the
stricter sense). To it belong the great philosophers Lao Tzu, 604-
517 B.C., and Kung Tu-tzu (Confucius), 551-479 B.C. Confucius, who claimed to be a "transmitter" rather than an
original thinker, edited the already ancient books and records
of China—including the record of rites (Li Chi). Music was
associated with the nature of things, the cosmic structure and
rhythms, as evidenced in *The Book of Changes (I Ching)*. The
actual records of ritual, as such, in performance are necessarily
lacking. We can only point to the evidence of continuing (as
they have survived in some places to the present day, apparently
almost unchanged) agricultural festivals and dance dramas, and
the ritual, associated with music and stylised gesture, of religion
proper in the temples.

The unfortunate destruction of books and musical instruments
ordered by the Emperor Shih-huang-ti at the end of the Chou
dynasty was followed by reconstruction under the Han dynasty
(206 B.C.-A.D. 220). An Imperial Office of Music was set up,
and no fewer than eight hundred musicians were attached at
one time to the Emperor's establishment. Then, in the first century A.D., Buddhist monks reached China, and a further impulse
was given to ritual, musical, and mimetic presentation. In the

late fifth century highly stylised dance, dramatic in kind, had become established in Confucian centres. A surviving hymn of six stanzas shows that dancers performed for part of the song. Holding a flute or wand in the left hand, and a pheasant's feather in the right, they took up thirty-two positions in each stanza. To appreciate the " mimesis " involved, we must remember that the Chinese speech is based (broadly) upon a limited number of monosyllables. According to the inflection or direction of pitch (neumes) given to it a monosyllable has varied meanings. Level, rise, fall, and enter (which may all be paralleled in our own tongue), when emphasised led to melody and more strictly musical pitch. In the Confucian mimesis every attitude taken was based on the " neume " of each word, and hence repeated the " tune " suggested by each word. The words, the music corresponding to them, the dance portraying the word and its music, were unified.

It is worth while considering such a precise and developed art form; it may help us to appreciate in some way the intricacies of Chinese theatre in the fuller sense. The much earlier *Record of Rites* had already stated the theory, " Poetry expresses the idea; song prolongs the sounds; dance enlivens the attitudes ". Such subtle and hieratic (or symbolic) presentation is an element in theatre often overlooked; but the producer who considers will find himself often, even in Western theatre, imitating the dance ritual. " Fitting the action to the word " is a more subtle and far-reaching concept than appears at first hearing.

Other influences reached prosperous and comparatively peaceful China during the first centuries of our era. From Samarkand, from Persia, from India, came various artistic techniques; performers arrived, whether for trade, as refugees from the disturbances of war in their own countries, or spreading their faith, as did the Nestorian Christians. The Empire was of considerable extent in the period of the early Middle Ages (in Europe) and as many centuries earlier all roads had led to Rome, so now (for half the world) all led to China. During this period the theatre (from the eighth century onwards) is clearly in being —at Court, as marionettes, and in other popular forms. The Mongol invasion was disastrous in some ways but the Yuan dynasty gave fresh encouragement to theatre. Restored Chinese rule in the Ming dynasty continued to support drama.

Finally, during the last dynasty of Imperial China we face the

D

intruding European influences; but, contrariwise, the influence of China on the west (even in the " chinoiserie " of the eighteenth century) has been considerable, whether in the (rather ineffective) imitation of Chinese music in such operas as Weber's *Turandot,* or the increasing study of Chinese philosophy. Under the Communist regime the Chinese theatre in general, as we shall see, seems likely to survive, together with traditional dance and music, even if much of the religious ceremonial from which it originated is no longer celebrated in its fuller forms.

2. *The Development of the Drama*

Dramatic origins in China resemble those of ancient Greece. Ritual celebrations gradually introduced a sequence of events. (Cp. developments of " tropes " from the Mass in mediaeval times.) Music and ritual dance were combined with the telling of a story by the later sixth century A.D., and the wearing of masks was adopted about the same time. (Cp., again, classical Greek practice.) Luckily, sculptures and reliefs give some idea of the actual attitudes, besides the fact of performance. Dramatic art is naturally so evanescent that one is happy when some material remains are found. But, in the nature of things, it is not until the theatre is fully established that such remains, the result of possibly a millenium of development, *are* deposited. The parallel development of music and theatre is instanced in the reign of the Emperor Hsuan-tsung (713-756) who established six standing and eight sitting orchestras indoors, an outdoor assemblage of thirteen hundred players, and (more important to us) in the second year of his reign organised a troupe of three hundred actors, known as the Pear Garden, a kind of dramatic academy. Further, he is reputed to have written music for the theatre. Actual plays survive, in part at least, from this period.

Not without significance for the theatre is the use by T'ang poets of the short lute for accompanying singers. They composed music which itself told a story—such as " The Last Battle of Hsiang Yu ", with onomatopoeic percussion and " slides " to illustrate the course of the fight. More important is the move (to be parallelled later in Japan) towards a popular theatre, in addition to the dignity and carefully controlled conventions of Court drama. Again, puppets had been the earlier form of theatre for the people, in general. Actors appeared as " live puppets ", a striking if false anticipation of some twentieth century western theories of dramatic "direction" which picture the director as a manipulator and the actors, ideally, as his puppets. Accompanying song varied, but from these origins, including the dance element in the drama, the "opera" or music drama of China which we know today developed. The ordered tones, however, used the four "neumes" noted earlier. Speech inflection and musical pattern were interdependent.

During the period of Mongol influence, operatic drama was encouraged, the emperors favouring the introduction of new instruments and new musical scales. So much so, that the drama was called, with its ensemble, the "music of the Mongol" dynasty. From this period date the earliest complete surviving operas, either in the Northern style which used seven note scales originally and accompanied the voice by the short lute, or the Southern, with five note scale melodies and support from the cross flute. "Mixed" forms also occur. The intricate method of communicating the events, characters, and moods of the play, in the highly developed form of theatre which emerged during the thirteenth and fourteenth centuries, has remained to the present day. Mime, recitative, and metrical songs, are mingled in the comprehensive plan of the Northern style, and the melodies themselves, associated with a certain verse-form and scale-mode, "set" the dramatic situation. (A rather crude parallel would be the semi-comic use in a light modern "musical" of a particular theme or style of music—sentimental valse or "beat" music—to typify a certain character's approach—or the pianist's illustrative accompaniment to the old silent film.) Similarly, in the southern style which, during the Yuan dynasty, became more important, a particular theme is assigned to a particular situation.

During the Ming dynasty still longer plays appeared—upwards of thirty acts being used by Wei-Liang-fu, usually involving the alternation of narrative declamation and metrical songs. The *History of Lute Playing* has a hundred arias alternating with dialogue. At the end of the dynasty men were formed into separate troupes and the falsetto voice became a necessary part of the classical opera. The whole mode of vocal attack, however, varies from our western conventions.

During the nineteenth century the "opera" which had received few new impulses, was modified by more popular elements, possibly from folk culture, such as three-four time and simpler melodies. This new opera was known as *ching-hsi*, songs of the capital, the so-called Pekin Opera, the most commonly performed " classical " drama at the present time.

3. *The Plays*

The plays are lengthy; their themes well known; the real Chinese audience tireless but critical. Absence of scenery allows the writer to move from scene to scene, and to construct episodic dramas of limitless scope and plot. The actors are able to select and perform chosen scenes which are in a sense complete in themselves.

Such a scene is " Where three roads meet ", an episode from *The Generals of the Yang Family,* a fourteenth century folk-tale dating, in the present operatic version, from the nineteenth. The good general Chiao Tsan has been exiled, accompanied on his way by two guards, who intend him harm. He puts up at an inn, kept by a muscular fellow who serves " good " people, but dislikes corrupt officials and rogues. Following the general, secretly, is the young man J'en Tang-hui, who is determined that no harm shall come to the exiled patriot. The inn-keeper Liu, discovers that the guards intend to kill the general; unfortunately, when J'en arrives his questions lead the inn-keeper to imagine that he also is against the general. J'en, on the contrary, is suspicious of the inn-keeper's evasive answers. In the night, Liu, the inn-keeper, enters J'en's room to discover what he is doing; J'en, wakeful, leaps to meet his imaginary assailant. Then follows the battle in the dark, one of the most brilliant pieces of acrobatics and miming ever devised for the theatre. There is no dimming of stage lighting. Darkness is evoked by the movements of the actors. Finally, Liu's wife and the general enter. Complete confusion finds resolution as a candle sheds light. All is well and all explained.

This example may serve to show how the essential techniques are yet part of the action; all arises inevitably—the sword sweep that just misses, the actors moving away, feeling, probing with their weapons, running, jumping . . . one slight error and the whole scene would fail.

There is no clear distinction between tragedy and comedy in Chinese classical drama, although elements of both (as we understand the terms in the west) naturally exist. The spirit of comedy, revolt, and carnival, is typified by the adventures of

Fig. 8.—Monkey—an impression of the make-up of the character as presented by the Classical Theatre of China.

Monkey, who assaults not only the stronghold of heaven but the home of the great philosopher Lao-Tsze. Such plays are based on fairy tale and legend, early songs and stories. One episode may be mentioned. Sun Wu-k'ung, the Monkey King, attended by his monkey followers, is now Guardian of the Peach Orchard in the Palace of Heaven. Celestial Maidens arrive to gather peaches

for a feast which is to be given by the Mother of Heaven.
Monkey learns that he is not invited. Angry, he sets out and
arrives at the banquet room. No guests have yet come—but the
banquet is prepared. He gorges himself, gathering together more
food for his followers. On the way back, he finds the home of
Lao-Tze, who has gone to the banquet. The Monkey King explores and finds the golden pills of immortality. He determines
to secure immortality, and although one would be sufficient,
munches them " like fried beans ". Pleased with himself, he
returns to his earthly home, the Mountain of Flowers and Fruit.
The Lord of the Universe sends four armies to punish Monkey
—but despite their magic powers, the " big and clumsy "
heavenly spirits are defeated. The monkeys sing a triumph
song.

The mimetic fights, the headlong acrobatics, dialogue that
breaks into chant, and then into song, are all contained in such
an episode; but the attention is held by the Monkey King.
Mischief, animal joy, cunning, the embodiment of monkeydom
in movement and gesture, all are somehow conveyed by the
actor. Particularly expert are tiny facial motions, grinnings, never
grotesque, but always pointing unmistakably the thoughts and
feelings of the monkey, while his fighting is a demonstration of
athletic poise and physical fluency. Some commentators see the
monkey stories as a personification of more serious revolt against
religious authority, but he is rather an animal Harlequin, the
Saturnalian spirit of Misrule; the corresponding impulse in
Greek drama might well be Aristophanic comedy with its free
" guying " of gods and rulers, which exists alongside serious
reverence and tragic approach.

One of the loveliest episodes, given by the Classical Theatre
of China on their visit to Britain in the 1950's, an episode almost
equally successful on television, is the scene from the sixteenth
century opera *The Jade Hairpin*. The girl Ch'en is in pursuit of
her lover P'an who has been forced away to sit for his examina-
tions. Defying social convention, Ch'en seeks him, comes to a
river, and asks an old boatman to help her to catch up with
" someone ". The boatman teases her, and there is a scene
where he cross-questions, demands money, and finally insists on
singing a song. At last, he rows her right up to the lover's boat.
The action is presented without scenery; all the boat movements,
the balance of the girl as the boat rocks, the gliding motions when

they strike out into the stream, are shown by the actors solely through bodily posture and carefully timed action, one working with the other in response to the boat's imagined swaying and progress. When the scene is recalled to mind, one *sees* it with boat, river, and background scenery, so vivid is the communication of the actors.

New operas are still written. *In Yentang Mountain,* composed and directed by Hsu Chu-hua, won a first prize in the first National Festival of Classical and Folk Drama held in the

Fig. 9.—Military leader in Chinese classical drama.

People's Republic of China. Here Meng Hai-Kung, a popular Robin Hood leader, successfully resists the general sent against him, who falls back to defend Yentang Mountain. The final assault gives an opportunity for the acrobatic skill of the actors; men hurl themselves into the fort over the wall from a standing position with an ease that seems impossible.

The examples have been given from the current repertoire of the Pekin Opera. But this is only one (if the most typical and vital) of the dramatic conventions. Earlier, and less popular, " operas " are still acted and revived, sometimes by amateurs. All over China, each province has (or had) its own style of drama, with varying forms of theatre, but, typically, the simple stage projecting into the auditorium or the temporary platform. Performances celebrate festival times such as the New Year. " Throughout China there are perhaps a hundred different types of drama. This is popular art in the best sense. Its national audience is enormous. Between player and spectator, moreover, exists an intense and close relationship." (Peter Townsend : Peking Opera—the classical theatre of China; p. 5 of booklet *The Classical Theatre of the People's Republic of China.*)

The survival power of the Chinese theatre is manifest. When the Chinese People's Republic was established in 1949 many of the actors of the Peking Opera flew to Formosa. There they established the Operatic Group of the Republic of China, and have a repertoire of two hundred and fifty plays. They have also toured in Britain. They are probably more traditional in emphasis, concerned to retain *all* the existing dramatic repertoire, performing the " original plays " exactly as they have been in China " for countless centuries ". The worship dance at the start of their performance, in which a " heavenly official descends to welcome and bless the audience ", was notable. So, too, the dance of the flower-scattering angel.

4.   *The Theatre and its Conventions*

The classical theatre based, as the Greek, on earlier temple performances, used a stage jutting forward into the audience, with two rear entrances, one to each side, and a canopy, reminding us in general (though there are many minor differences) of the Elizabethan setting. Similarly, along behind the stage ran the green room—the equivalent of the Elizabethan tiring house—crowded with props and equipment. Diagrams show this clearly.

This kind of theatre still exists, according to authorities, in the provinces, along with many other acting places. China is a land of theatres of one kind or another. In the larger towns, there has

FIG. 10.—Principal dancer on formal platform in the Lotus Dance.

been a tendency to draw back the stage to a proscenium opening, following western example under the general impulse (given by the middle classes some years ago) to imitation of European ideas. However, such modification in no way alters the essential nature and conventions of the theatre, and, now that the West itself is returning to more flexible forms of staging and Eastern nations are beginning to realise the value of their own cultures, this trend may well cease.

There is no scenery as such. Hence, just as in Elizabethan theatre, there can be rapid and immediate transition from place to place. A curtained background and similarly curtained doors, left for entrance, right for exit, provide the formal setting. Furniture is more symbolic than representational—a table may represent an altar, a platform, or even, if jumped over, a wall or other obstacle. Chairs are used similarly. In the style of classroom drama, three covered by a curtain may be a bed. Simple arches may be the gates of a city. A character with a whip is riding an imaginary horse; with an oar he is in a boat. Painted panels may carry stylised pictures of mountains. Typical is the use made of flags; waved violently, they convey a rushing wind; with waves painted on they denote water; banners show (grouped in fours) the advancing army; with appropriate inscription, military ranks. Lanterns, umbrellas of state, shop and inn signs, scrolls, fill the stage with significance.

But if the " setting " is thus simple, the actor's task is demanding, developed far beyond (perhaps) anything else in the skills of theatre throughout the world. He *is* the performance. He is isolated on the bare stage. Every move and gesture must combine meaning with the grace that marks achievement, and the technique that is simply the best and surest way to fulfil intention. He must be singer, dancer, acrobat, mime, and, beyond this, an actor in the fullest sense. Long and strenuous training starts when he is young; his build and talents will determine the rôles on which he will specialise. For seven years or more he must learn patiently. Broadly, there are four types of part: *cheng,* men in general; *tan,* women; *ching,* strong male characters, faces painted as masks; and *ch'ou,* broad comedians, whose work may involve animal impersonation and knockabout farce. The female impersonator has a special importance; as in Elizabethan drama, the male is probably able to give a more " artistic " and subtle presentation of the part, and is preferred by many to the women now allowed to work with the male actors. (Mingling of the sexes was not encouraged by Confucian thought, though clearly allowed at some earlier periods of the theatre.)

Normally the " falsetto " voice is used by all characters except

the "robust" character men and the comics. We have already
noted the importance of the music and its "modes". The

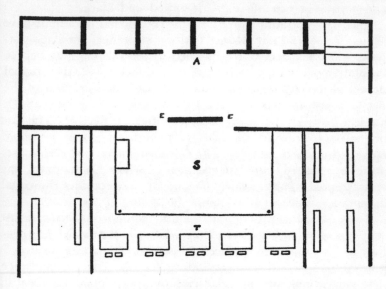

Fig. 11.—Sketch plan of Chinese stage and "tiring house" (A).
E—entrances.   S—Stage.   T—tables for audience

orchestra sits or kneels on the stage. The importance of various
percussion instruments, each of which may indicate a particular
type of action or emotion, has also been indicated.

Costumes are essentially theatrical—i.e. they do not aspire to
historical or naturalistic accuracy any more than did those of the
Elizabethan or Restoration theatre in our own country. It is first
the broad effect and, after that, the symbolism that is important;
communication theatrically is the aim—not a history lesson or
photographic visual reproduction. Adapted from the styles of
early dynasties they may show through their colour rank and
character, the yellow of an emperor, the red of a high official, or
the black of a humble or rough person. The equipment of a
general is perhaps the most elaborate stage costume in general
usage; a head-dress of glittering jewels and spangles may be sur-
mounted by pheasants' plumes six feet long; four pennons are
carried from the back, fixed between shoulders; tigers' heads
glare from padded shoulders, and the legs seem winged with
great panniers attached. Yet all this is functional, not useless,
finery; the pheasant plumes sway in victory, the jewels gleam

and menace in the ferocity of the fight, the whole costume lives in the dance movements of combat as something wholly animate and hostile, or can quiver with hatred and alarm.

The sleeves, traditionally long for ceremonial occasions, have acquired a special significance and use in drama. For stage purposes white silk sleeves are fastened to the existing garment, to facilitate movement, which was found difficult with the original sleeves of the costume. The skilful use and manipulation of the sleeves is just one part of the actor's technique. " Sleeve-play " is an intricate, lovely, and vivid essential of his art. The use of the sleeve to mask an aside or to indicate a tear is simple enough, but A. B. Scott in *The Classical Theatre of China* lists no fewer than 107 movements, each of which has its particular and accepted significance. (The student may consider the equal importance of sleeves in Nō dances in Japan.)

There are, of course, besides the fully equipped theatres, many simple stages, such as exist everywhere in the world for performers who move from place to place. The " matting theatres " put up temporarily can reproduce for the country audience the conventions of the classical, or more popular, theatre. (Note similar temporary theatres in Malaya.) The permanent theatre is, as it were, a part of the temple structure (from which drama emanated) taken away and set up by itself. The temporary platform represents the temple group (with its priest in still existing practice in Malaya) touring round the communities of its district. In the holiday fairgrounds of Hong Kong were tented performances of Canton opera in 1961.

5. *Influence and importance*

The influence and vitality of Chinese theatre in its various forms (and their related conventions) is more real than sometimes apparent. As we shall see it dominated dramatic development in the Far East and parts of Indonesia. Stationed in Labuan, Mr. Dennis Yare saw a few years ago regular visits of Chinese opera companies from the mainland of Borneo. In the west the cult of " chinoiserie " might be disregarded were it not that opera in the west took over (as in Weber's *Turandot*) Chinese melodic themes. Clearly, it would seem likely that in full theatrical presentations (such as opera and ballet) Chinese influence (from corresponding dramatic expression which involves song, dance, and recitative) would be strongest. However, popular Chinese folk story drama, not so developed perhaps technically, has made some progress in rather " westernised " versions. The famous play *The Chalk Circle* was rewritten by Brecht as *The Caucasian Chalk Circle,* a kind of bridge betwen eastern and western drama. S. I. Hsiung, using typical conventions, gave us *Lady Precious Stream.* But the most powerful impact is not so much the actual dramas as their methods of presentation. The simplified stage of Brecht, the mimed situation, the imagined setting, the stylised yet vividly " real " movements and conventions of *Lady Precious Stream* helped to restore to theatre in the west valuable aspects of presentation. Finally, it is no accident that children's plays have been written in Chinese convention, with flexible stage, frankly theatrical appeal, property man in full view, and orchestra on stage, an honest " let's pretend " which gives children a way to fuller theatrical experience than the deadening imposition (at too early an age) of western naturalism, which is not merely alien to the child mind but also bars a full appreciation of the essential nature and functioning of theatre. " Lyrical realism " can easily surpass " naturalism " in truthful presentation of life.

Perhaps the best comment on the importance of Chinese classical theatre was made by an actor, reared and trained in the best skills of " picture-frame naturalism ", after he had seen the " opera " in performance: " Well, now I've got to rethink all my ideas on what theatre is—from the beginning."

CHAPTER V

JAPAN

We are lucky nowadays in that we can study the origin of
drama from rituals "before our very eyes", to quote a
comedian's catch phrase. Films have been made of Japanese
"rice rituals" acted today (1961) just as in past times, beneath
the slopes of Mount Fujiyama, and attended (as, indeed, is only
fitting) by farmers, schoolmasters, and officials of the agricultural
co-operatives. Despite fertilisers, insecticides, and machinery, the
Japanese veneration for life itself, the hidden powers of fertility,
has not diminished—indeed, why should it? So the Shinto priests
still invoke the favour of the Powers on the village rice fields.

Into the courtyard of the shrine are driven the decorated
oxen; girls have the place of honour, with their bizarre head-
dresses, for they, as women, are guardians of the mysteries of
reproduction. Then, as we watch the screen, we see and hear the
man who represents (perhaps one should say in whom resides
the spirit of) the rice god sing the verses, while the chorus of
girls reply, and the young men beat out a rhythm on percussion
and drums. Then, on a special plot, the girls enact the planting
of the rice; on this ritual planting the fertility of the whole
valley depends. In some rites the planting is carried out
mimetically, just as in part of this drama, which follows, the
young men awake the forces of life, as they dance, flourishing
sticks. There is not a vast difference in kind between such a rite
as this and the Dionysiac worship of ancient Greece.

Or we may watch (again on film) the slaying of the puppet
who represents a hated mediaeval war lord. As he died he had
sworn to return in a swarm of locusts to ravage the crops, even
as he had destroyed them when alive. Round his puppet figure

the villagers move in a slow threatening dance. The priests exorcise the ghost. The puppet is carried from the shrine to the valley river, killed with sword thrusts, and then thrown into the stream, where the straddled body, turning grotesquely with extended limbs and painted eyes staring balefully, is caught and buffeted away by the waters. With him is washed away the curse for another year.

Or we watch a festival dragon dance—the ever relevant story of human endurance against the beasts of death and evil, now a popular " variety " act, ingenious, amusing, and dextrous. From all these elements come the theatre and dramatic traditions of such a nation as Japan, and, other things being equal, of many other nations.

1. *Historical Background*

The culture of Japan has always been dependent on that of the mainland. Earlier inhabitants were gradually superseded by later immigrants. Thus the more primitive Ainu, who once occupied a great part of the main island, are now only a small remnant. Chinese records show that by the Christian era there was a settled government, although during the first century there was still war with the Ainu. Korea was conquered in the second century, re-opening contact with China, and possibly introducing Chinese literature and writing. The government was hereditary, and was re-organised (under Chinese influence) in the sixth century. Local chieftains were replaced by governors appointed by the central authority under the Mikado. In the seventh century Korea broke away, but at the same time Buddhism made progress in Japan, culminating in the eighth century, when a Buddhist priest became prime minister. It was then not unknown for the Mikado to resign his throne to a successor, and himself enter religion after some years of rule. In the late eighth century the capital was established at Kyoto, where it remained until 1868. Up to the mid-eleventh century, Japan was comparatively peaceful and prosperous, and shared in the literary culture of China. Then two noble families of Imperial origin struggled for supremacy; for a hundred and fifty years this eastern parallel to the English wars of the roses went on. Normal trade and cultural exchange with China lapsed. Struggles of powerful territorial families, whose power had gradually grown through military rule, continued for centuries, even after the arrival of Portuguese traders and Jesuit missionaries in the sixteenth century. (At the start of the eighteenth there were a million Christians in Japan.) Hideyoshi gained total power in 1590, nominally as regent.

An invasion of Korea in 1592, aimed at the Chinese, although devastating the country, was defeated in its main effort. In 1600 Iyeyasu obtained power and established a settled government which was to last for two hundred and fifty years. Means were found to control the great families, and possible sources of opposition were dealt with severely, the Christian minority among them. The effectual ruler of the country was the Shogun, the commander of the army; the Mikado had been for centuries more or less dependent on the feudal nobles who fought for supremacy. In 1867, the Mikado, with the abolition of the feudal system, once more assumed authority, aided by the revival of Shinto, which gave him divine status as the descendant of the sun-god. Both Buddhism and Confucian thought exist alongside the " state " religion of Shinto; indeed, a man may well observe all three. Shinto (as we have seen above) is largely concerned with the relationship of man to the natural forces with which he must co-operate to live.

Drama in Japan (as will be noted from this brief summary of history) has thus necessarily a disturbed development, and is all the more fascinating therefore. The disruption of the Chinese culture, which, blended with native practice and religion, had fostered education and the arts previous to the tenth century, meant that theatre had to be re-established almost artificially by patronage (as often seems almost inevitable) with interesting results.

2. *The Nō drama*

Here is a form of theatre closely associated with the feudal aristocracy which led to the Shogunate rule of the fourteenth and fifteenth centuries, so much so that when the Shogunate was deprived of power in 1868, the Nō drama suffered temporary eclipse. Its intrinsic merits as a form of theatre ensured revival, and it has exerted some influence in the west. Yet it is still an art of " caste ", appealing to one part of the community. (One may consider whether such *particular* social appeal is not almost invariably true of theatre, though more explicit in Nō drama.) When it first emerges in the fourteenth century it is clearly the product of many previous centuries of dramatic activity, and its connection with Buddhist ritual can be seen in its themes and ideas. It draws for its plots on Chinese and Japanese stories and myths, as well as from temple ceremonies and folk-lore, including dance and festivals. The Nō are written in Court colloquial speech of the fourteenth century. Interludes (comic and farcical), which were acted at the same time, are in vernacular of the sixteenth century. At the beginning of the seventeenth century the Nō drama perfected its qualities as a form of theatre, and has changed little since. Hence the retention of earlier language in its dialogue.

3. *The Nō " theatre " and its conventions*

This demonstrates in several of its features the reliance of early theatre on preceding religious occasions. It shows also a refinement of symbolism and convention, such as may be developed from ceremonial and liturgy. Further, we see the close alliance of music, dance, and action.

The Nō stage is a raised platform. The audience sit on two sides of it. Over it is a temple roof. The pillars which support it have special significance in performance; thus the front right pillar is that of the second actor; diagonally left rear is the station of the first actor. On the right along ths stage a small balcony is placed for the ten singers. At the back are accommodated four musicians and two stage assistants. Most important, from the rear of the stage runs backwards at a diagonal a passage way, narrower than the main stage, about forty feet in length, which leads to a curtained entrance by which performers reach the main stage. This passage way may symbolise the approach to earth from heaven, or the journey to the spirit world, and is thus part of the acting area. The close alliance of natural and supernatural is pre-supposed by the material and origin of the plays.

There is no scenery in the accepted sense. A light framework of wooden posts may support a roof to represent a temple or house, or even a palace. (One is reminded of the " mansions " of mediaeval drama in Europe.) A stylised pine tree decorates the back wall of the stage. Costume is rich and decorative. The central part of the play is the temple dance from which the drama originated. (Compare, again, early Greek tragedy and its stress on the " orchestra " or dancing place.) For this the first

E

actor wears a mask. Other actors do not wear masks. In theory there are two actors only. But they may have many companions; as in some other early dramatic forms, however, the first actor is very much the maker of the play; the second is far below him in importance. This does not mean, of course, that Nō drama is undeveloped; it is simply theatre which has taken a different course as it moved from its primitive origins, a course which has resulted (it *might* be held) in a far higher form of theatre than the crude naturalism of the West! The main stage, eighteen feet square, is of highly polished cypress. This carefully maintained surface is important in performance. The orchestra is simply a transverse flute, two hand-drums, and a larger drum struck with two sticks.

As in ancient Greece or mediaeval England the sequence of plays occupies some time—ideally a whole day—starting either at (say) ten in the morning, and lasting until four or five o'clock, or commencing at one in the afternoon and ending in mid-evening. Five pieces are given, with a finale. In addition comic relief is provided by the interludes or *kyogen*. The Greeks separated their tragedy, the serious business of religion and the approach of man to the powers, from their comedy, social re-adjustment, the freedom, under the aegis of the god, to make fun of all established communal authority. The Japanese in the Nō play sequences interlaced the forms; here between dramas of high subtlety and such moving power that even today the unimaginative and wilfully matter-of-fact spectator is awed, are acted the most rumbustious farces, in which no great person is safe from mockery—the lord, the monk, the gods themselves (cp. the treatment of Dionysos in *The Frogs*), as well as drunken servants, boasters, scolding wives, amorous old men, all are alike exhibited in their laughable absurdity and stripped of false pretensions.

Even the selection of plays, however, is guarded by rule. The programme should contain, according to modern classification of the plays, (1) The god piece, (2) The battle piece, (3) The wig piece, (4) The mad piece, (5) The melodrama, (6) The finale. An example of the " wig piece " is *Ha-goromo* (The Feather Robe). A fisherman discovers the " feather robe " of an angel, without which she cannot be received in heaven again. After some effort, she persuades him to return it to her—and in reward dances for him the dances performed in heaven. This brief description exemplifies features of the Nō—the revelation of the chief actor

as a superhuman being, and the dance which is the foundation
" theme " of the drama.

4. *The Plays*

We shall take as our example *Nakamitsu,* an early fifteenth
century play by Seami.

At the start Nakamitsu appears on the " bridge ", announces
his name, and tells us that he is on a journey to the monastery
in the mountains of Chiynuzauzhi, where the son of his master
Mitsunaka is placed to study, but, alas, is wasting his time. He
speaks the words as he journeys to arrive at the main stage. At
the monastery, he is met by his son, who is page to Bijiyau, son
of Mitsunaka. Taken to Bijiyau's apartment, he orders him to
leave at once, without telling the monks. They arrive back at
Mitsunaka's palace. (All this, of course, merely by movement
about the stage.) Mitsunaka now tests his son. He is unable to
read the scriptures, to make verses, and knows nothing of music.
The chorus chant describes the father's anger and the shame of
so disobedient a child. Accompanying the action, they tell how
Nakamitsu stops his master from killing the boy. But Mitsunaka
then commands *him* to kill Bijiyau. In a moving scene which
follows, Mitsunaka kills his own son rather than his lord's son,
the two boys each being willing to die.

In the second part, an abbot comes bringing with him the still
living Bijiyau, who has been in hiding at his monastery. He reveals Nakamitsu's action, and pleads for pardon for the son—
" If only as an act of piety towards the soul of Kauzhiyu, curse
not thy son." The chorus describe the subsequent rejoicing, and
Nakamitsu is asked to dance, telling of the sadness in his heart,
although the gay throng see only " the rhythmic waving " of his
sleeve. The dance over, the chorus describe how Nakamitsu gives
good advice to Bijiyau as he leaves with the abbot. They go, but
Nakamitsu watching the departing palanquin thinks how he will
never again see his own child carried home.

This play, by one of the most famous of the early Nō writers,
has interesting features. The absolute loyalty to the lord, the
need to preserve the dynasty, may seem to us strange—though no
stranger than the problem confronting Orestes. The apparent
return from the dead of the son is the nearest that the play comes
to the supernatural. Normally the introduction from the bridge is
performed by the second actor, not the first as in this case.

Similarly, the dance of joy and despair, which is the central theme of the play, is performed by the First Actor (as usual) but still essentially as a human being, though he has risen above selfish human considerations. The rhythmic movement of the dance is accented (against the stately dignity of the gliding movements) by the tapping and stamping of the feet on the polished floor, and accompanied, of course, by the percussion of the orchestra. The use of the sleeve (mentioned by Nakamitsu as he dances) evokes the typical gestures of the convention. Words themselves suggest something of the movement, as Nakamitsu likens the departing prince to a " water-bird that has lost its mate " and describes its action fluttering over the waves, an idea taken up by the chorus after the mention of the sleeve, " hither and thither fluttering in the wind ".

The Nō plays (Nō means talent—and the drama therefore displays the " talent " or skill of the performer) number some two hundred and fifty in the present acting list. Altogether about three hundred are known of pre-seventeenth century origin. The music is, of course, an integral part of the presentation; the recitative inclines to a note of constant pitch; a measure of eight beats (or sixteen sub-beats) is kept (or felt as a basis) through the play, and words have to be fitted to these beats. The verse, however, may be alternate seven and five syllable lines, so that the voice has to syncopate and vary across the basic rhythm. The scale is five note in the major third form.

5.　*The Kabuki Drama and Theatre.*

The Nō drama, though deriving from Shinto shrine rites allied to Buddhist thought, became in feudal days more and more an art for the aristocracy and a court entertainment. In the early seventeenth century a woman dancer, attached to a Buddhist shrine, developed the dances, with a flute and drum accompaniment, as a popular form for the ordinary people. A women's acting company was formed but later suppressed as " immoral " in 1629. One recalls that about the same time a company of French actors was driven from the English stage because it used women in women's parts!

The new theatre, known as Kabuki, persisted, although the young men's company which succeeded the women's was likewise closed in 1652. The impulse was strong; playwrights worked for the new form and it has remained ever since a popular theatre of dance-drama. During the early years the samisen was added to the orchestra. Kabuki, while basing still very considerably on dance, gradually drew to itself all kinds of stories and material, especially the actions associated with the puppet theatre (see below). It adopted, too, a form of presentation, in which action is accompanied by a chorus which chants the story, used by the marionette theatre. The social cleavage between the

Fig. 12.—Late eighteenth century Kabuki actor in make-up and costume.

feudal warrior class and the townspeople was instanced when samurai were not allowed to attend performances. It was essentially a bourgeois theatre. Companies have toured the West with success—the element of plot and story is stronger, and the scenery and décor more appealing to most audiences, than the austere beauty and somewhat remote thought of the Nō drama proper.

The Kabuki stage, like the Greek classical platform, is wide and shallow; from the mid-eighteenth century a revolve was added which is now essential to the planning of the presentation. As in the Nō theatre there is a long gangway to the stage, but, whereas in the Nō this leads away to the " other world ", in the Kabuki this raised walk runs along from the back of the hall to the stage, level with the heads of the audience. (It will be remembered by those who have seen some Japanese films.) Characters enter by this, and may sometimes withdraw here from the main stage to stand aside or to comment. The settings (as often in bourgeois theatre) are exact and correct, but one is never over-conscious of them, since a full furnished Japanese room seems almost a stylised convention to our eyes. On the other hand, the music and effects are supplied by an orchestra seated on stage behind a lattice work on stage right. If the play is in the style of the marionette *joruri* a reciter and a samisen player sit stage left. Two stage assistants are also in view, though supposedly invisible. They had in olden times to hold a bamboo with a lantern, so that an actor's face was lit clearly, and to follow the actor round.

6. *Conventions of Kabuki*

Masks are rarely used, except when a Nō play is performed

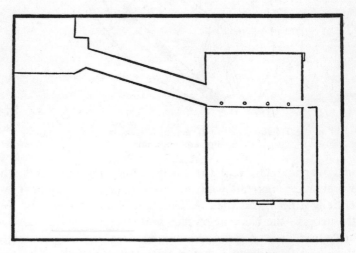

Fig. 13.—Sketch plan of stage for Nō plays.

(the complete break with the other form of theatre was, of course, impossible). On the other hand, facial make-up is elaborate when stories from classical times are presented, much in the manner (to our eyes) of the Chinese " opera ". Similarly, rich brocaded costumes are used for such plays, while for " everyday " dramas plainer dress is used.

The performance has an air of " variety " about it. Selections are given from several plays; certain scenes have attained such popularity (whether from subject matter or the technical skill involved) that they have names and an identity of their own. Further, dances form separate items on the programme. One might say that Kabuki is a skilfully popular form of theatre; potentially it appeals to all of the audience for some of the time, to some of the audience for all the time, and to the more enthusiastic (such as myself) everything appeals all the time!

The Kabuki recognises three main types of drama:

(a) the history (jidaimono), with a sub-class of plays of specially powerful action, the aragoto—these constitute the highest test of the Kabuki actor's skill;
(b) the sewamono, melodramas with popular appeal, and
(c) the shosagoto or dances.

7. *The Marionette Theatre*

Puppets and puppet plays are found the world over, developing from, with, or even before, the regular drama which employs live actors. Sometimes it is also suggested that they represent a further development of theatre art—and that the ideal human actor would be one who could make himself absolutely subservient to the director who " pulls the strings ". While such a view is hardly to be taken seriously the limitations of puppets in one direction open up advantages in others. The immobile faces and strong features take on, according to their lighting and angle, the most vivid expressions of hate and love. By linking with strange inherited images in the subconscious they evoke, and are charged with, the fears and living force of the spectator. The most terrifying and beautiful film I have ever seen consisted of the " camera eye " wandering among the puppets assembled by a Dutch collector. They were not working; they were still; but a whole world of human and superhuman emotion was evoked by them, not merely for the sensitive, but for people of very materialistic minds and unimaginative outlook.

Nor need one wonder at this evocation of feeling. Puppets,

just as drama itself, developed functionally as a part of religious practice. We have seen above an example of a play with a puppet used to cast out a curse. In the temples of the ancient world images were made that could move their heads and limbs; primitive tribes have similar idols. As George Speaight remarks, " the dividing line between charlatanry and religious drama was, perhaps, sometimes finely drawn ".

In the far east Buddhist stories are still presented by the puppet showman, especially in Burma and Indonesia. In Europe Bible plays were performed by puppets long after they ceased to be acted on the " live " stage. To introduce the topic of puppets through the drama of Japan is, however, appropriate, for here for centuries they occupied a particularly important place in entertainment, moving away from the more narrowly religious aspect of drama. Puppetry is, of course, revered as a means of spreading popular information; in the far East the puppet-master is respected as an educator; and in the West the social and educational power of puppetry has been widely recognised, not in any narrow didactic sense, though all kinds of work can be taught through the medium of puppetry, but as a significant cultural activity. But in Japan, puppetry as an art form attained a perfection and detailed theatrical efficiency almost unparalleled elsewhere.

Undoubtedly, the marionettes of Japan influenced and inspired the Kabuki which adopted so much of their material and practice. The same wide shallow stage is used, but these puppet presentations have quite elaborate setting. The puppets are two-thirds life size. The " director " or puppet-master wears a cere-monial costume, and stands in view of the audience, as do the manipulators. Assistants wear hoods to indicate their " functional " invisibility, and (clearly) to avoid intruding their own facial play into the action. The story is chanted by five singers to the music of the samisen.

When, as described above, the temple rituals developed into the Nō Drama, which became more and more an exclusive art form, the marionettes, taking their origin from the same religious themes and practice, naturally became more important to the ordinary people. Moreover, the puppet company is (in a sense, despite its high skills) more mobile and less demanding in its requirements than the " live " theatre. Naturally, too, the marion-ettes linked with the activities of wandering story-tellers, and adapted popular stories into their own repertoire, adding, to religious myths, folk tales and Buddhist legends.

With the rise of the Kabuki in times of greater tranquillity, the marionettes became less popular, though they still exist today, with perhaps even heightened skill and beauty of performance. Much of their dramatic material was taken by the Kabuki companies.

The easy transition from puppets to live theatre, or vice-versa, in the human approach to drama, may be seen in schools today, where children make their own puppet plays, or themselves move imaginatively in free dramatisation. It is, perhaps, no accident that one of the most popular stories, films, and plays—in the delightful " audience participation " version of Brian Way—is the story of Pinocchio, the puppet who became a human being.

8. *Characteristics and influence*

Their drama shows the ability of the Japanese to assimilate and to use in new creation the cultural attainments of other nations. We have noted their contacts with Korea and China both in drama and, inevitably, music during the period of the sixth to twelfth centuries. Through Buddhist influence Indian drama also reached Japan. Dance drama of Sanskrit origin came in the early eighth century, and ancient Indian music dramas now unknown in their land of origin are still played, such as those of Siladitya. At the unveiling of a great image of the Buddha at Nara hundreds of foreign musicians took part in the rites, and the instruments actually used on that occasion are preserved in a treasure house at that place. Significantly, authorities tell us that Japan is the only place where a fruitful marriage between eastern and western forms of music is in being. The same, I believe, may be true of drama, not because the Japanese have necessarily a higher form of theatre than other Eastern countries, but because they seem able to work more flexibly and in some way to appeal more widely in their artistic achievements. Paradoxically, though, much of the appeal and influence of eastern theatre in the west has been achieved by the apparently remote and unwestern Nō theatre.

Chapter VI

INDIA

India is not one country, but many; not one culture, but several, blended, superimposed, rich in tradition and thought, yet preserving through its dominant religion—Hinduism (or more correctly the religion of the Vedas)—an ability to communicate and share ideas throughout the vast subcontinent to which the name " India " is somewhat loosely applied, now sub-divided into " India " and " Pakistan ", where the Mohammedan religion, brought by the Mogul Emperors in the Middle Ages, represents the contribution of a ruling class in the last great wave of invasion or migration before the gradual British dominance.

The caste system in Hinduism is (as Radhakrishnan tells us in *The Hindu View of Life*) itself a witness to the taking over of conquered populations and their preservation within a common social pattern. (We may note also the frequent difference of skin colour as between high and low caste.) So the Gods (regarded by the educated Hindu as manifestations of the One) are drawn from many sources, and from differing cultures. So, too, the central theme of re-incarnation, the gradual approach to the " end of the journey ", the atttainment of fulfilment and peace, shows the same pattern of reconciliation, differing lives in differing circumstances gradually resolving in a harmony. " The individual life is not a term but a series." (op. cit., p. 89). Similarly the history of a race moves in rhythmic progress. " Hinduism is a movement, not a position." (p. 91).

Radhakrishnan notes the Upanishads as presenting a spiritual religion to supersede the cruder ceremonial of the Vedas; when controversy threatened to destroy the impulse of the Upanishads with dogmatic dialectic, the Buddha called for adherence to the essential simplicity of truth and the moral imperatives implicit in life. The *Bhagavadgita* restored to the pure in heart the realities of the spirit when over emphasis on scholastic argument obscured the way.

So Indian religious thought has balanced, through the centuries, the varying ways to God and Truth, establishing an ever richer tradition. Note, finally, two further simple statements from Radhakrishnan which may state more vividly the general basis of " Indian " culture. " Caste . . . was the instrument by which Hinduism civilised the different tribes it took in." (p. 75.) " Hinduism adopted an attitude of comprehensive charity . . . It accepted the multitude of aboriginal gods . . . outside the Aryan traditions and justified them all. It brought together into one whole all believers in God." (p. 28.)

1. *Historical background*

India is strategically situated as a world centre—not a route, or landbridge, as Palestine, but a meeting place of cultures. From early times it has traded with the west by sea or by overland routes; to the North, through passes and over tableland it has had relations with the great eastern cultures we have already briefly considered; its own civilisation and beliefs have at times been powerful in Indonesia, as in the nearer Burma and Malaya, meeting again, as we round the S.E. corner of Asia, with the Chinese influence from the North.

We are nearing our own traditions and heritage as we consider India, and not merely because dominant Hindu influences derive from the Indo-Germanic peoples who gradually invaded and penetrated India in the centuries before Christ. Whereas we used to think of these invaders as overcoming a somewhat primitive Dravidian population, we now know that powerful and complex cultures—possibly of a higher order than that of the invaders—were established in the Indus valley at much the same time as the civilisations of Mesopotamia and Egypt settled around the Euphrates and Nile. So Sir Mortimer Wheeler notes a coffin burial of the Indus civilisation at Harappa as dating from the third millenium B.C.—the date of the great cemetery at Ur of the Chaldees described by Sir Leonard Woolley. (*Archaeology from the Earth,* p. 124.) This Indus civilisation, spread over a wide area, had well planned towns, buildings of immense height and strength, and an established way of peaceful, fruitful, living which endured for centuries, ruled, perhaps, paternally by elders and wise men.

But, just as centuries later Northern barbarians were to sack peaceful unwalled towns of the Roman Empire, so now from the North came warrior Indo-Germanic peoples; their ideals are perpetuated in the name they gave themselves, Ary'ya—warriors, whence our own term for themselves and ourselves, their kinsfolk, Aryan. Excavations show the process of destruction. As we have seen, however, the lighter skinned warrior caste, as the new kingdoms were established, imbibed something of another way of life and from the intermingling of cultures and races the Hindu civilisation developed. The Aryans, entering from the north-east, gradually spread to the east, driven on by succeeding waves of immigrants as well as by their own natural desire for conquest.

Existing kingdoms in the vast area of India, however, gave way only slowly. The size and the fertility of the country, the stiffening resistance (and even expanding wealth) of the Dravidians (as for example in Southern India, where their language, Tamil, remained in face of the Sanskrit of the invaders) made the process a long one. Indeed, in the end a kind of equilibrium was established in which empires were built up within the subcontinent, and not imposed by external pressure. While in the Rig-Veda the Aryans appear as a pastoral people, free from caste, by the time of the Code of Manu (900 B.C.) the fourfold division of caste is accepted. Nor must we forget that in addition to the invaders and the conquered societies there were many smaller and more primitive groups (who are still represented) living in less accessible regions.

During the late fourth century B.C. Alexander led from Greece his almost abortive invasion of the Punjab; in 302 B.C. missions were still sent from Greek rulers to Northern India. Coins, remains, sculptures, show some intermingling of Hellenic and " Indian " culture and styles. From that time on, especially in the days of the Roman Empire, trade was developed between east and west, with settlements and marts (again explored by Sir Mortimer Wheeler) on the Indian coastline; the sea route was probably safer and cheaper than the land journey for merchants. In B.C. 259 Asoka was crowned in Pataliputra (near Patna), king of a powerful state, the territories of which he extended and ruled with almost idealistic care. Pillars and rock inscriptions have been found as far as the Nepalese frontier, at Delhi, Peshawar, and Allahabad. His edicts make provision for planting trees, irrigation, medical care (for animals as well as men) and advocate religious toleration. The comparative peace and prosperity of the period is evident. In the fifth century B.C., taught Gautama the Enlightened (or Buddha), son of a king ruling near the borders of Nepal, whose reforms we have mentioned above. Asoka, who was to all intents and purposes " Emperor of India " (so entitled in the Oxford Companion to English Literature) gave much of his time and energy to the spread of Buddhism and sent missionaries to many parts of India and to other countries.

Succeeding kingdoms moved centres of power to other areas of the sub-continent. We must note the accounts given by Chinese travellers—Fu-hian (in 399 A.D.) and Hiuan Tang (629-645 A.D.). It was during the first six centuries of our era that Hindu culture may be said to have flourished most typically. During this period the great dramatists lived, the arts of dance and mime, all that is preserved today as of value, reached their fulfilment, delicacy, and sensitivity.

From the year 1000 onwards, history is repeated. Now it is Mohammedan invaders who press in from the North East, under such leaders as Mahmud, grandson of a Turki slave, gradually taking more and more of the land despite alliances of Hindu rulers, until the establishment, centuries later, of the Mogul Empire brought the process to an end. Not, however, without the same ultimate compromise, when Akbar partly by force of arms, partly by friendly overtures, established an Empire based on sound civil administration, religious toleration, and patronage of Sanskrit literature and culture. Yet the religion of the " conquerors " remained, in this instance, distinct. Islam persisted as such. The basic cleavage is perpetuated today in the existence of Pakistan as a separate state.

Subsequent penetration of India by Western nations, the gradual absorption of Western thought, and the final independence of the subcontinent need not be stated in detail. What must be noted is that Hindu thought and culture are again reviving and exerting power. From the time of the English Restoration theatre onwards, India has fascinated and mystified the West. Researches of scholars into her language and traditions have given much information about our own language and culture;

translations from her holy books, and the impact of Kalidasa's drama *Sakuntala* (first translated by Sir William Jones in 1771), the growing influence of Indian philosophy, her art, and her moral ideas, all indicate the fertility and vitality of India today. And by India we mean, essentially, Hindu thought, literature, and (here) theatre, although in vast areas there are many variants, many minorities, and a great Mohammedan population in the neighbouring state of Pakistan.

2. Early drama

The various tribes of India had their rituals and dance dramas as other peoples. These may be studied in Frazer's *The Golden Bough*. The early cultures, such as that of Harappa in the Indus valley, have necessarily left few records; but in sculpture and cult objects there are evidences of dramatic rituals, dance, and entertainment born from the festivals of the community. From the common stock of religious celebration, stories of Gods and heroes associated with such occasions, dance and music so much a part of Indian life, drama proper and theatre evolved. The existing material shows clearly its earlier ritual and religious associations. The Dravidians needed music and dance for their fertility cults; these, we are told, persist with the Tamil speakers of the south and their folk music. A tradition that each note of the scale originated in an animal cry suggests primitive mimesis and association with nature forces. The Indus Valley civilisation has left figurines of dancers and one of a woman drummer, clear indication that dramatic rituals had developed into dance and entertainment.

Chant which can still be heard in Indian temples today was introduced with the Aryan invaders and the earliest prayers, hymns, and ritual expressions, represented by the Rig Veda. The precision of Indian art-form is implicit in such religious archetypes; correct intonation was essential in the simple three note scheme of the early hymns.

The subsequent development of the extremely complex Indian musical system and such matters as the " supernatural " effect of chant may be studied in *The Pelican History of Music*, vol. I For us, the fact that the Sanskrit word for music, Samgita, has the wider meaning of " art and science of singing " associated with music and dancing (op. cit. p. 26) is not unimportant. Hieratic hand movements were implicit in the restrained dance

allowed. These formed a starting point for the more developed
dance forms of the south—the strictly classical and religious
Bharata Natyam; it was the non-Aryan God Siva who became
the Lord of the Dance. Music and dance are continually found
in connection with religious ceremonies, court occasions, and
private entertainment. There was a development parallel to the
Western distinction between tragedy and comedy—" Marga "
was music " composed by the gods " which might liberate man
and free him from the cycle of lives; " Desi " (lit. " regional ")
was music for communal entertainment—a matter of here and
now.

Just as in Greece the " goat songs " drew gradually upon the
varied myths and stories of other Gods and men, so, in Southern
India, the musical dance dramas incorporated the stories from the
great epics—the Ramayana and the Mahabharata (400 B.C. to
400 A.D.). The resulting dance dramas are still found today with
the Kathakali of Kerala in the south.

The two centuries before Christ were a period of development
and consolidation, followed by expansion, largely inspired by
Buddhist zeal and missionary effort. The influence of the Greeks
may have introduced further musical instruments, as seen on
Greco-Buddhist sculptures in Gandhara (Kandahar); Indian
musical influence spread into other countries of the east; but so
also did their drama proper by the same religious dynamic. Our
earliest records of written plays are fragments from the work of
Asvaghosa (c. 100 A.D.) found in the sands of central Asia. Already
we have a developed form, for these are imbued with Buddhist
faith, and indeed might almost be termed " propaganda " plays.
Finally, the first writings on theatre, drama, and music, are all
contained in one work, regarded by Hindus as a classic of
authority. Just as we in a sense look back to Aristotle as a foundation figure of Western theatre, so Indians regard Bharata, the
traditional author of the *Natyasastra,* as the founder of classical
music, and he (or the writing associated with him) is our authority for the practices of classical theatre.

3. *The Theatre*

Why select one period of Indian drama and theatre for special
consideration? Because one must choose, and, choosing, fix on
that which represents the highest achievement in the theatre of
a country, that which has guided its development since, and that

which is felt today to be important for the future. Just as we study the theatre of Greece in the age of Pericles, and revive its dramas, or re-establish its theatre forms, just as we perpetuate the practice and achievement of Shakespeare, so we may value the conventions and methods of classical Sanskrit theatre from the early centuries of our era. Ujjain in west-central India in the fourth and fifth centuries was the capital of a powerful kingdom. Here the greatest of classical playwrights lived and worked at the court of King Vikramaditya. In his day, suggests Arthur Ryder, " Ujjain . . . stands worthily beside Athens, Rome, Florence, and London, in their greater centuries." He regards the era as a renaissance comparable with the time of Shakespeare.

Bharata gives us instructions for the construction, organisation, and performance, of the theatre. He is concerned with the whole scope of drama; indeed, his work may be said to epitomise the total view of theatre which we accept in this book, for he deals with dancing, costume, and music, as well as with the composition and production of the written drama. Later practice in theatre was largely determined by the work, just as, in a sense, Aristotle was regarded by many as establishing necessary canons of theatrical art in the west.

Theatre buildings as such were not usual. Here, Indian classical practice illustrates the origin and nature of theatre. In early times a performance is staged where an audience may be gathered. Later, just as in Greek theatre, the small shelter or hut is erected for the convenience of actors; then gradually the more elaborate and dignified background and apparatus develop. But in classical Indian theatre we still have no permanent theatre building; and (as we have so often noted) " scenery ", picture setting, as such, is not of the nature of theatre at all, in striking contrast to costume and make-up. Even in the costly court performances envisaged by the plays of Kalidasa, based on the practice described by Bharata, the stage and equipment are erected for the specific performance, much as a special setting was provided for the Court masques in England much later; though in the latter " scenic " display was, contrary to Indian practice, dominant.

The performance was, again as in Greece at first, staged for some particular festival or celebration, either in the palace under Royal patronage, or within the precincts of a temple.

4. *Conventions and Disciplines of Performance*

Since themes were taken from stories of the gods and demi-gods, as in most " classical " theatre, or from the manners and customary reactions of the middle class citizens, characters were, as in ancient Greece, recognisable types, established gradually, maybe, but none the less firmly. The protagonist or hero (nayaka) is of noble or kingly status; the antagonist is brave and strong, but evil (pratinayaka); the heroine (though not necessarily of high birth) must be beautiful and intelligent (nayika); others involved are the hero's companion (the man of pleasure and worldly wisdom) and the manservant. The function of drama to provide an outlet for criticism of authority, or authority misused, is illustrated by the vidusaka—a greedy, illiterate brahmin, a man of high caste who is unworthy of his birth and himself a comic contradiction. (Cp. the comic mandarin in Chinese theatre.)

Performance of the play was often linked with an introductory variety entertainment. This exhibition of human ingenuity and diverse accomplishment in song, dance, and acrobatics, was followed by acts of worship and the prescribed ritual which took the audience into theatre proper, based in religious observance, man's life in relation to the powers of the world. Then came a benediction and the prologue to the play.

Costume was careful, not merely beautiful in itself, but also (as in the Chinese and Greek theatres) symbolic of the rank and profession, nationality and nature, of the character. Misery and distraction could be, as on the Elizabethan stage, indicated by torn and dirty dress; the sober garment might show the man of religion; if an ascetic he might wear rags; in contrast the dress of princes and demi-gods glowed with colour and ornament. Preparatory to setting up auditorium and stage, religious rites would initiate the work of establishing what was, in effect, a temple for the powers that guided the dramatic art. The auditorium was divided by pillars into sections for the castes, and rows of seats were provided, the king, or other patron, and his attendants sitting in front. (Compare the situation of the High Priest of Dionysos and civic dignitaries in Greek classical theatre.) At the back of the acting space on the stage ran a curtain which masked off an area to be used as dressing rooms; here, too, " noises off " and the voices of gods who could not be presented on stage were

F

produced. As in the Roman theatre, the stage was decorated with reliefs and pictures; there was no scenery; the action took place before the curtain.

It must be noted that strict instructions were given as to the measurements and proportions of the building. No detail was ever overlooked in the *minutiae,* the exquisite care, typical of Indian artistic endeavour.

Properties were used, despite the absence of scenery, although these were essentially objects which were integral to movement and action, swords, staves, and so on. We do hear of special elaborations and " working " apparatus, such as an artificial elephant in a play about Udayana. In general, however, the actors indicated properties by subtle and stylised gesture, the significance of which was known as a recognised convention by the audience—picking flowers, chasing a butterfly, mounting a horse—methods which merged into Indian dance and mime techniques, and were part of the essential training and skills needed by the actors.

An interesting comment on race mingling, and its relationship to caste, is found in the skin painting used (in theatre) to indicate the origin of characters. Those from the north-west, where the Aryans and Greeks had invaded, were painted reddish-yellow; so were men of the high castes—brahmins and royalty; characters from the Ganges valley and two lower castes were coloured dark brown; while the Dravidians from the south, as well as members of the smaller and less civilised tribes, were black.

As in mediaeval England, when professional actors emerged, companies moved round from town to town finding work where they could. They doubtless had a good idea of the festivals and occasions at which they would be welcome and planned their seasonal activities accordingly. As with the *commedia dell'arte,* each troupe had an actor-manager, who was also the producer of the plays, the sutradhara. He usually appeared in person at the start of the play to introduce the performance. He had an assistant manager, the pariparsvika, and a large company would also contain a stage manager, the sthapaka, who worked (be it noted) under the director, and whose duties involved the actual construction of the stage and its running. We note, of course, that women's parts *were* taken by women—except possibly, in broad comedy. In short, the classical Indian theatre in its general principles had achieved a pattern and established working

methods which the Western theatre would not reach for another
thousand years or more.

5. *The Plays*

These were of various kinds, which may be roughly approximated to equivalent dramatic approaches in other parts of the
world. The " resolution " of the conflict (or " happy ending ") is,
however, an accepted convention. (The student may like to consider this in the light of Hindu philosophy and religion.) The
nataka is the highest form of drama, the hero being a king or
demigod; this corresponds to the Greek " tragedy " (which may
also have a not *unhappy* conclusion). As in early Western theatre,
the number of main actors must be limited—in this case to five;
the play should have at least five acts—and not more than ten.
The subject was normally taken from existing religious myth or
story. The comedy of town life was represented by the *prakarana*,
though the characters might still be of high rank—brahmins or
wealthy merchants—and the plot was the business of the dramatist himself.

Short farcical plays about the activities of low-life rogues are
found in the *prahasana*. The character monologue or *bhana,* in
which the " rake " wanders through the town and converses with
the people he meets (who, of course, do not actually appear on
the stage), would be familiar enough to patrons of nineteenth
century English music hall, granted the change of locality and
manners. Two other forms of drama are the *samavakara*, which
we might term a " mystery " play, since it is concerned solely
with gods and demi-gods and the *natika,* which is a lighter
version of the *nataka*, dealing with the love affairs of the hero—
a " romantic " play. (Students should note that the parallels suggested are only very approximate—but have been found helpful
as a starting point for study. We are dealing with a culture and
assumptions rather different from our own, even though we may
feel on more familiar ground than with the Chinese theatre, for
example.) The greatest plays were produced before A.D. 1000.
We have already mentioned Asvaghosa. The full development of
the drama in the fourth century brought Bhasa and Sudraka,
and in the fifth the highest achievement of Sanskrit drama came
with Kalidasa. Later writers are Visakhadatta, Bhatta Nara-
yana, King Harsa of Kanauj (besides plays of court life he wrote
also a drama of religious interest on a Buddhist theme) and

(ranked second only to Kalidasa) Bhavabhuti. In the last named, there is a slightly artificial dignity of theme, a conscious effort to repeat past glories, and to maintain the grandeur and high seriousness of theatre. Inevitably, later dramatists seem to imitate and to echo rather than to create anew, a frequent tendency in theatre. (Compare the "literary" blank verse plays of the Victorians which attempted to revive Elizabethan emotion and power.) The Mohammedan invasions only confirmed this already inevitable trend.

In a sense, theatre, allied to liturgy, always tends to retain older traditions and impulses. This does not mean that it is out of date—simply that it exhibits the permanent and enduring human situations among outward flux and social change. (Note how dramatists such as Eliot and Sartre use Greek "myths" for contemporary drama.) The two-fold task of theatre is illustrated by the language of the plays. Kings and high caste characters speak in Sanskrit, now almost a liturgical language (compare the sadness of the fifth century Sidonius at the decay of classical Latin speech in Gaul, although it was retained in the church), while the bourgeoisie speak Prakrit, the vernacular current in the early centuries of our era. The eternal and the contemporary are thus symbolised side by side. In general, dramas were written in prose, with lyric passages and choral interludes.

Examine Kalidasa's greatest play, *Sakuntala*. The outward plot is a simple enough "fairy" story (in the popular sense), taken from the first book of the *Mahabharata*. King Dushyanta, out hunting, sees the lovely girl Sakuntala, marries her impulsively, giving her a ring before he returns home. She follows, but loses the ring while bathing. The king does not recognise her and she returns to the forest bearing Bharata, founder of a great race. A fisherman finds the ring in a fish; taken to the king, the ring breaks the spell, and he goes to find Sakuntala.

After the benediction in the name of the eight forms of Shiva, the stage-director enters (as customary), summons an actress, praises the taste of the audience (again customary) and exhorts the company through the actress to do their very best. The actress sings, and the stage director pretends that, spell-bound by her voice, he has forgotten the play to be shown. This gives the chance for a repetition of the theme, and for the stage director to set the scene where

the bounding antelope allures
The King Dushyanta on the chase intent.

(Quotations are from Monier-Williams' version, fifth edition, 1887.)

Act I shows the entry of the King with his charioteer, the action of driving being conveyed in mime. When the king is about to shoot at the antelope he is prevented by hermits who tell him that the animal belongs to them.

> Now heaven forbid this barbed shaft descend
> Upon the fragile body of a fawn
> Like fire upon a heap of tender flowers!

The King stops, and is invited to the hermitage. The journey in the chariot is again shown in mime. Then the king removes, as befits one entering a place of penance, his ornaments. Hearing voices, he stands aside and sees the hermit's daughter and her friends enter,

> In palaces such charms are rarely ours;
> The woodland plants outshine the garden flowers.
> I will conceal myself in this shade and watch them.

The traditional dress of the hermitage is indicated by the king's words—

> The lotus with the saivala entwined
> Is not a whit less brilliant; dusky spots
> Heighten the lustre of the cold-rayed moon;
> This lovely maiden in her dress of bark
> Seems all the lovelier.

Sakuntala moves round, tending the flowers and shrubs of the garden, which allow Kalidasa to build up the scene through his detailed observation and lyrical delight in the beauty of nature. Now a bee follows and worries Sakuntala; again the whole action is mimetically shown with tiny fluttering movements. The king takes the opportunity to show himself. The girls stand shy and silent. Sakuntala does not speak but her companions are more talkative and tell the king of her real birth and parentage. The girls discuss whether hospitality should be given to the stranger. Sakuntala, attracted by him, tries to cover her feelings by a show of indifference. A voice behind the scenes warns that King Dushyanta is near and that a wild elephant has been driven into the hermitage gardens. The king is annoyed that his companions have broken the peace of the place; now, when the girls should seek safety, Sakuntala delays; her foot has been hurt by spear grass and her mantle entangled in a bush. The girls help her to free herself, and the king is left to say (with a typical Kalidasa image)

> My limbs drawn onward leave my heart behind
> Like silken pennant borne against the wind.

Act II opens with a long speech (rare in Indian drama, where dialogue is swift and exchanged in lively fashion, save for special purposes, such as the comedian's " turn ") by the " jester ", who is, much in the vein of Touchstone, tired and bored by forest life. " We toil on from jungle to jungle, wandering about in the paths of the woods, where the trees afford no shelter." Now, in addition to all the weariness and the boring hunting talk, there is more trouble—the king has fallen in love. There is a wordy argument between the general (who enters with the king and tells the praises of hunting) and the jester who angrily tells him, " Wander about from forest to forest till some old bear seizes you by the nose ". The king also does not want to hunt, and confides to the jester his love and the beauty of Sakuntala. (" Tired of sweet dates, and longs for sour tamarinds ", comments the listener on such love for a country girl.)

Serious passages, in praise of beauty, are in poetic form, while the comments of the jester are in prose. Hermits enter to beg the king to stay with them because they need the hero's protection. Immediately he has consented, messages arrive from his mother summoning him to attend an important ceremony. In this dilemma the king sends his confidant to take his place. " Let me travel in fitting manner," says the jester, adopting a kingly strut. As he goes, the king is anxious that his secret shall not be told, and assures his friend, " I am going to the hermitage solely out of respect for its pious inhabitants and not because I really have any liking for Sakuntala . . ." " Don't distress yourself—I quite understand," briefly and ironically answers the jester, and the act ends.

In Act III, however, the lovers reveal their feelings indirectly through the writing of a poem and the help of Sakuntala's friends. They part unwillingly. A prelude to Act IV, where girls talk as they pick flowers, tells us that the king and Sakuntala are now married. (The dramatic economy of Kalidasa is notable. Marriage was implicit in the preceding act—but nothing is actually said; the essential climax of love accepted and reciprocated is sufficient.) The friends are worried that the king will forget his bride after his return. Kanwa, her guardian, approves the marriage, and prepares to send her to the king. There is an appealing scene in which the girl says good-bye to the nymphs, the animals, trees, and friends, of her forest life, and finally to her guardian.

In Act V we are shown the king at his court tired and entertained by court poets (whose voices are heard from behind the scenes), and by the singing of Court ladies. It is clear, too, that the king *has* forgotten; he wonders why he is so moved by a love song, although he is aware only of the jealousies of his queens. The deputation from the hermit Kanwa, Sakuntala's party, arrive, but when the king is confronted by her, he cannot remember the marriage, although he is once again moved by her beauty. Comments a worldly wise attendant, " Who else would hesitate for a moment when good fortune offered for his acceptance so beautiful a woman?" Sakuntala feels for the ring, the token of their love, but it has gone. A priest counsels " a middle course "; the lady shall stay with him till after the birth of her child; the baby may have the marks of empire (the discus) on his hand.

The prelude to the next act shows two policemen dragging in an unfortunate fisherman, asking where he has obtained the king's signet ring. He tells them he has found it in a carp. The superintendent of police admits that at least one part of the story is true—the man is plainly a fisherman; his own nose tells him that; but as for the rest of the story! A walk round the stage indicates the journey to the palace. While the superintendent is inside the constables plan in serio-comic fashion how they will put the fisherman to death; their superior returns and tells them to set the fisherman free. " What do you think of my livelihood now?" asks the fisherman, accepting the money which the king has sent him. After more verbal sparring, all go off to drink at the nearest wine shop.

Act VI shows the descent of the nymph Sanumati in a
" celestial car ". Sakuntala is dear to her. She wonders why the
great spring festival is not being celebrated by the king. Two
girls who are looking after the garden plants enter and talk in-
formatively (a repeated device). Kalidasa, however, always introduces particular interest even for lesser characters. The mango-
blossom, the sign of spring, has opened. One girl calls to the
other. Together they dedicate a bud to the god of love. The
chamberlain enters angrily. The king has forbidden all mention
of spring festivities. The girls protest that they have only just
been sent to care for the pleasure grounds; the official explains
that the king has now remembered his marriage, and is heart-
broken at the loss of his wife. The king enters and a long scene
shows his effort to conduct the business of the kingdom. A portrait of Sakuntala is brought to him, and the device by which the
king is roused from his inactivity and dull grief—the work of
Indra's messenger—is beautifully written and moving, even in
translation. Varying emotion, details of allusion, despair which
cannot avoid constantly adding to its own pain by thought of the
lost wife, are all skilfully presented; the dramatic interest does
not lessen, even though there is little direct action until the ex-
citing conclusion.

The final act starts with the journey, through the air, of
Matali and the King in Indra's car. The progress of the travellers
is indicated by mime and words . . .

> We are moving
> Over pregnant clouds, surcharged with rain; below us
> I see the moisture-loving Chatakas
> In sportive flight dart through the spokes . . .

There is opportunity for descriptive speech as they near their
destination. Arrived in the sacred grove, they meet a child,
whom the king discovers to be his son. The reunion with Sakuntala is made. The dialogue in the scene of recognition has the
reality of immediate experience. There follows the " religious "
climax of the plot, the presentation of the king to the sage and
demi-god Kasyapa, who, discovered on a throne, reveals why and
how he caught Sakuntala away to protect her, and explains the
curse that caused the king's forgetfulness. The child is named as
a kind of " messiah "; mankind shall hail him as King Bharata.

Kasyapa blesses the king with the promise of abundant harvests
for his people, and the king himself gives the final prayer

> May kings reign only for their subjects' weal;
> May the divine Saraswati, the source
> Of speech, and goddess of dramatic art
> Be ever honoured by the great and wise . . .

6. *Drama and the Life Process*

Kalidasa was a man of education and learning, widely
travelled in his own country, a master of both the existing theory
and the practice of drama and poetry, as well as a philosopher
and a man of broad religious sympathy. Yet his main (and constant) pre-occupation was with the life of Nature, its unfailing
beauty, its varied form. The fourth and thirteenth cantos of *The
Dynasty of Raghu* describe journeys over most of India, as does
the lovely poem *The Cloud Messenger*. While his work is " full
of the Himalayas " (Ryder : op. cit. x) the details of flowers and
plants, the scented warmth of Kashmir, are also his joy. Yet it
is in events, the human beings who are involved, that the
dramatist must be judged. And Kalidasa is not wanting; his portrayal of women and children, sometimes lightly amusing (" So
handsome a man must be good," argues a handmaid in *Sakuntala* to her friend), more often catching moods of tenderness,
hope and utter despair : his presentation of childhood true, with
its boastfulness, loyalty, and directness. (" I want my mother,"
the little Bharata tells the king, and when the latter suggests they
go together, " You're not my father—Dushyanta is," objects the
boy.) But the overall effect is greater than any analysis can indicate. Nature, gods, and mortals, blend into a unity of life
which theatrically was caught and communicated in imaginative
simplicity of presentation and the gorgeous colouring of the
stylised costume; ceremonial and life are married in the celebration of creative love.

> She is God's vision, of pure thought
> Composed in His creative mind

says the King of Sakuntala. (" How the women must hate her,"
comments the jester.) One remembers Marlowe's hero in similar
situation, " Ah, fair Zenocrate, divine Zenocrate . . ." All life

is truly one—from plant to gods—and all is therefore intensified; Kalidasa's feeling for Nature dramatically reinforces the emotions of his characters. As Ryder points out, the instinctive Hindu belief in reincarnation helps the dramatist; rivers, mountains, and trees, have their own reality; they, too, are happy in their life, and share the action. Yet this is a feeling which many in the western world have come to share, whatever their beliefs. There is, too, in Kalidasa's natural allusion, the " wealth of observed fact " dear to the more " scientific ".

His other plays are *Malavika and Agnimitra,* and the *Urvashi,* where Indian insistence that drama must result in fulfilled life alters a tragic story to reunite the lovers. The *Malavika* is perhaps his earliest play, since when the stage director announces that the audience has asked at " this spring festival " for a play by Kalidasa his assistant protests. Shall they neglect the work of such famous authors as Bhasa, Saumilla, and Kaviputra, for that of a modern writer? " Not all is good that's old," says the director. " Well, it's your responsibility," answers his assistant. This first effort is a light story of court intrigue. The *Urvashi* dramatises a famous Hindu story—the love of a mortal for a nymph. Hindu opinion rates the work highly, though the refusal to face the inevitable " tragedy " of such a love does not please some Western critics.

Let us recall finally that in essence all Indian classical drama is operatic. We can no longer envisage, save in occasional revival, the total effect of music, dance and mime; as we study scripts we must recognise that (as acted) dignity and (especially in such a difficult plot as the *Urvashi*) conviction would be added in performance, as well as tenderness and detail.

7. Indian Drama today

The greatest period of Indian drama was over before the Mohammedan invasions. The withdrawal of the patronage of the ruling classes merely confirmed, in the years following 1000 A.D., the lack of vital impulse. Kashmir preserved the performances for some time, but today, in the direct line of tradition, only in Malabar does a caste of actors and performers, the Cakkiyar, preserve something of the heritage. Remote Manipur, however, has retained dance and ritual almost unimpaired in its folk-culture. Performances by its actors have now been seen outside their native state and have given a new impulse to interest in

Indian theatre. With the revival of Hindu culture in the nineteenth century, the *Sakuntala* was again performed, for the first
time (in Bengali translation) in 1857. It had previously been
translated into English and other European languages; performance was not fully successful, since a script is only a part of
theatre's needs, and until the conventions and conditions of presentation were known the actual play could hardly be revived,
even supposing western performers could learn the necessary refinement of technique, music, and dance. We must be content to
share the achievement and to be a good audience whenever we
have the chance to see Indian theatre, in whatever form, dance,
classical drama, or even film, where much of the delicacy and
convention is sometimes retained.

In such writers and dramatists as the great Rabindranath
Tagore (1861-1941) the influence of the classical theatre lives
again. His poems, which show much of the same appreciation
of nature and childhood as Kalidasa's, have been translated into
English. But he also wrote plays—*Chitra, The King of the Dark
Chamber,* and *The Oleanders,* besides furnishing a preface to
Sakuntala. What we may call the *total* achievement and
approach of classical Indian theatre is still very much alive, even
if, perhaps, awaiting reincarnation, just as Greek theatre in the
west. And over the wide view of the centuries it occupies a
central and unassailable position in theatre and dramatic form.

Chapter VII

SOUTH-EAST ASIA AND INDONESIA

To gather together this vast region, its varied cultures and peoples, its myriad islands and migrations, as if it possessed a unity is, on the face of it, absurd. And yet it possesses in its variety a feature which distinguishes it from the more slowly changing and massive civilisations of China and India, the two great powers by which, or through which, pressure and rule has been imposed upon the even older peoples of the islands and the coast lands of Eastern Asia. It is an area of mixed cultures, susceptible to both Indian and Chinese influences, and latterly (though now probably less) to western penetration. The varied and quickly changing aspects of dance and drama are seen very clearly in Bali, that most creative and artistic of lands. A new integration may be possible through the establishment of Indonesia as a single " nation ", though within its boundaries a bewildering richness of tribal life and traditional cultures are found.

1. *Historical Background*

Burma is (roughly speaking) an extension of India, though its population varies from less civilised hill tribes to the highly developed Buddhist culture of the greater cities. The Burmese language in which secular works are written is akin to Tibetan, while the holy books are composed in Pali, the sacred language. Important philosophical and religious works are thus Indian in origin, the alphabet itself based on that used in Ceylon, introduced by Buddhist missionaries in the fifth century A.D. More than any other country Burma has remained the stronghold of Buddhism; the great temples and monasteries, tombs and pagodas, are known to most of us from illustrations. On the other hand, invasion from China was a constant danger in the middle ages, as well as conflict with Siam. In addition, civil war between petty states (if one can regard Burma in those days as sufficiently a unity to speak of "civil" war) went on inter-mittently. The establishment of single rule is comparatively recent, in the eighteenth and nineteenth centuries; British in-fluence aided the growing "Empire" against the French, and then British influence assumed control in the mid-nineteenth century.

As we can see, from Burma stretches a long peninsula (probing to the south and the territories of Indonesia) comprising various Malay States, now united in Malaya. The quiet, and graceful mannered, indigenous Malays, more akin to the island peoples of the Pacific, have to live and work with active and vigorous Chinese immigrants who form part of the continual outwards pressure from China itself along the seaboards to the south. At the southern tip lies the base of Singapore, mark of Western influence.

Before we move on further into Indonesia, recall that to the east and north of the Malay Peninsula lies Siam, with a mixed Mongolian and Indonesian population. Here, while Buddhism is the accepted religion, as in Burma to its west, native and earlier religions are (as so often) blended into the faith and practice of the people, while in the more remote northern dis-tricts Shamanism is found.

Siam is by its nature a buffer state, and as such separated British and French interests in the nineteenth century. Its posi-tion between contrasting cultures and powers is illustrated by the usurpation of the throne in the eighteenth century by a Chinese general, after the Burmese had devastated part of the country, including the capital. A minority of the population are Siamese; the rest are very largely Chinese—probably almost equal in num-bers—with immigrants from Malaya and the kingdoms to the east, Cambodia, Laos, and Indo-China in general. Moving on to those lands, we reach again ancient civilisations, powerful a thousand years ago, visibly evidenced in the great ruins of Angkor Vat. Buddhism came here also with the great mission-ary movement of the fourth century, but Buddhism is (as in some other countries) superimposed on animism and earlier religious beliefs. Chinese immigration is again significant.

The more recent history of these countries, following the removal of colonial influence, wars between Communist and other forces, and the resulting partition of territory, is only too familiar. In a sense, however, these struggles are, under a new regime, a continuation of earlier Chinese pressure, a perpetuation of a sphere of influence which has existed for centuries in one form or another. Certainly Chinese culture patterns (in drama, for example) have been powerful in these countries, just as the Indian drama has influenced lands further west, notably Malaya.

Looking again at Malaya on the map, we see its coastline facing part of the great island mass of Sumatra. From Sumatra the routes of communication are open south east to the other Indonesian islands, large and small, and to Bali, the magic land. The story of Sumatra is largely that of Java also. In the early centuries of our era, Hindu culture spread into the islands, leaving imposing remains of temples and cities. But, as in India, this civilisation was overcome by Mohammedan invading armies in the period between the fourteenth and sixteenth centuries. While in India Hinduism still remained the religion of the majority, save in the more northerly districts, where the invaders could impose their will more effectively, the populations of the Indonesian islands could not absorb the conquerors so as to retain Hinduism; Mohammedanism became the chief religion, as in Malaya also. There was, however, one part of Indonesia which the wave of Mohammedan conquest failed to reach. Just as its influence petered out before the vast populations of southern India, so it stopped short before Bali, separated from the Mohammedan areas only by a mile of water. Cut off from the land of its origin, here Hindu culture still prospers, transformed, variable, but always creative, with important results for theatre. In a sense any attempt to treat briefly of the many nations and cultures contained in Indonesia is an impertinence. Here are eighty million people or more, with two hundred languages and dialects, several nations far older in civilisation and (in some ways) artistically richer than ourselves; lands, too, where true aesthetic education and sensitivity is possessed by almost the whole population, beside whom we may seem crude barbarians, save in our finest achievements, societies in which, intelligence, sensitivity, agile strength and harmonious movement, are still more valued than crude physical force or massive destructive power.

2. *The Theatre and its Conventions*

In the space available, we can direct the student only to some outstanding features of the work of each area. In time, as knowledge grows, it is possible that the literature concerning the drama of each country will attain the bulk of that written on, say, the theatre of ancient Greece. Whether that will be desirable or not, each of these lands has traditions and work of importance. Far better, of course, if we come to know and to witness the *performance* of their great works of drama.

Theatre in Burma was helped by the conquest of Siam in the eighteenth century, when troupes of dancers were brought back. Dance is popular, as in most of the countries under review, the basic material being events in the life of the Buddha and local legend. At festivals dance dramas are given, often in temporary " theatres " of woven hurdle walls and thatch roof shelters. Burma is one of the few countries where the intimate connection of theatre with social well-being—and the necessity of some state encouragement—was recognised by the civil service; in the early nineteenth century a Ministry of Theatre was set up, even though this was in a sense a precautionary move, to safeguard due decorum in the presentation of Buddhist ideas and events. Further, the puppet theatre had a powerful political influence in the nineteenth century. The Burmese term " pwe " may be rendered " show ", an indication of the varied aspects of theatre in their land; thus the " Zat pwe " deals with the classical period of their history and Buddhist stories, presented in strict dance and ritual patterns, the performance lasting through the night. Splendid costume and songs enrich the performance visually and aurally. A climax is reached with a *pas-de-deux* (compare the solo dance in the Nō of Japan); the dances involve gestures which link with the attitudes and movements of puppets, vigorous and firmly held. A full orchestra accompanies the action and indicates mood and situation, with xylophones, drums and castanets.

One is slightly ashamed of the " electronic music " of the west, its rather feeble blend of differing " noises ", and the enthusiasm with which some " modern dance " groups have hailed it; here in Burma is the real thing—a complete fabric of sounds much more varied (and artistically patterned) than the most ingenious electronic machinery can fortuitously provide—accompanying fully developed dance. The " answein pwe " extracts the more humorous and clown-like passages from longer dramas to form a separate entertainment, the dancers being made-up almost as western clowns, with white faces, rouged cheeks, and eyes outlined in black. The "yem pwe" performed often by amateurs, is the Burmese equivalent (in intent) of our "pageants", using allegorical themes and a great deal of costume and procession. The "yokthe pwe", puppet shows (the figures are from two to three feet high), are not so popular. Much of their material has been absorbed by the live actors. More difficult (and yet theatrically important, for the student of dramatic origins) to appreciate are the "Nat pwe", spirit dances, in which various costumes are donned until all thirty seven spirits have been embodied, caught, and thus exorcised; before the altar the spirits are propitiated by means given to them to *enter* the ritual by "worshippers", no longer aloof as enemies. The dancers enter a trance-like state, during which the audience put questions to them, the answers being given by the "spirits" who possess the bodies of dancers. Lastly, there is the more modern "pwe zat" which utilises stories of general interest, flexible and more inventive; yet it keeps Burmese traditions, song, dance, and older stories from the puppet plays. The Shans in Upper Burma, less under Indian cultural influence, have interesting festival dances.

Thailand is a mature society, where "Khon" preserves a theatrical form derived from India, but more alive and vital than traditional Indian theatre today, preserving almost the oldest conventions. Themes and plots are mainly from the Ramayana. When Buddhism ousted Hindu beliefs, the drama survived, retaining the Hindu stories much as we view the tragic themes of ancient Greece, though more lightheartedly, rather as fairy stories than as serious "myths" of man's predicament. Again, we may note that theatre is closely linked often with the courts of rulers. Rama VI during his long reign from 1880-1925 encouraged the "Noble Khon" in palace performance, the royal family taking parts, the "corps de ballet" being composed of officials. Here survives an early, yet fully developed, form of theatre. Singers tell the story and announce the characters (contrast the Chinese convention by which actors announce themselves) while the orchestra, with its percussion and xylophones, dictates the pace, pattern, and interpretation of events. Certain musical forms are, as in the Chinese, appropriate to particular situations; some are magical—and not to be lightly executed. The dancers wear the long sleeves associated with other Eastern theatres. Animal characters, such as Hanuman, are necessarily involved in the plots of the dramas. Changing circumstances have not favoured Khon, since few can now afford the expense of a troupe of actors or the performances. Nevertheless, Khon does survive.

On the other hand, Lakon (La-Khon) has some kind of state backing. This is a dance drama performed by women, using stories and the general traditions of presentation from the Khon. Lakon Hai is " pure " dance, as distinct from dramatic plot and situation. Lakon Nok is dance which tells a story. Lakon Duk Dambon tells a story in dance and adds scenery. So Thailand shows all forms, from " pure " dance to full dramatic presenta-

Fig. 14.—Sumatran folk dancers.

tion. In their dance there is rich material, combat dances (popular and valuable as rehearsal and training in bodily agility), teasing dances, where a gift is offered and dangled as a bait, and alphabet dances, where ideograms are presented symbolically, showing at times Chinese and Japanese influence, for example in the use of the fan.

G

Curiously, however, modern popular theatre is derived, ultimately, from Muslim influence, though little of this remains, save in the derivation of its name, Likay, from the Siamese for "praise to Allah". Originally inspired by the chants sung in penance and praise linked with events in Mohammed's life, the dramas now retain only the prayer song; all the rest is in keeping with strong native traditions of drama, blended to satisfy. The plots are episodic; a story may continue night after night, going on to fresh events, at the discretion of the actors and audience; the conventions of the Khon and Lakon are used—as well as their plot material—but the actors also themselves talk and sing; ordinary human characters, recognisable portrayals of modern Siamese life, are included. Siam, to use its old name, is a land of theatre, dance and drama. It is no wonder that an attempt to establish "western" theatre petered out. The national drama contains in itself all possibilities of theatrical art, certainly as relevant to Thai life and character; further, it is a more highly developed theatre than our own, if one considers all its manifestations and technical expertise, its wide range of appeal and social reality.

Cambodia looks back to the ancient and powerful civilisation of the Khmers, who were responsible, among other massive and carefully worked architectural achievements, for the great buildings of Angkor. Again, dance drama was most powerfully supported and performed with precision at the King's court, as at the Royal Khmer palace in Pnam-Penh. Inscriptions relating to dance are found in eighth century remains, the main influences being either directly from India, or through Indian colonised Java; the religion of Cambodia was Hinduism—in the twelfth century as many as 600 dancers might be attached to a single temple—to which Buddhism was added. Their powerful empire, at one time controlling much of Indo-China, exercising overlordship of nearby islands, exhausted itself in over-lavish building by the thirteenth century. Again, conquerors carried off not material loot only but also the dancers themselves—a slight indication of the scale of values in the east—so that in the fifteenth century Cambodian dancers were abducted to Siam.

The prestige of Court ballet, preserved and developed through centuries, is still powerful. Girls underwent strict training, under a carefully planned discipline, not merely of artistic purpose, but also of moral purity. Cambodian dance drama involves an amaz-

ing flexibility of fingers and hands, as well as complete supple-
ness of body, which moves with an ease and expression unknown
in the west, where tensions and unnatural ways of living inhibit
bodily rhythm and co-ordination. Costumes are gorgeous, real
jewels shine against shot silks; gold ornaments hold glistening
gems. The general conventions are by now familiar to us; the
chorus chant the story, the orchestra accompany action, and the
plots are from the Ramayana; but new themes are included.
Thanks to the interest of France in this country, its dance is not
unknown to the west, attracting the attention, for example, of
such artists as the sculptor Rodin.

Neighbouring Laos shows the same kind of drama and dance,
but in its most refined and gentle form. Here again is Court
dance. There are also touring shadow plays in Thai style. Some
find the Laotian drama the most subtle and harmonious form of
theatrical presentation. Dancing is traditionally part of a girl's
education, often simple and reflective in theme as in the Twilight Dance, in which the girl responds to the beauty of a sunset. Simple words accompany such a dance; a song repeats the
central idea. Buddhism, again, is the main faith of the country,
and festivals which involve music and dance are frequent. Yet
the lack of energy which characterises their dance keeps Laotians
from achieving full theatre; they are content to welcome Thai
companies to do the work for them.

If we pass on, or back, to the islands of Indonesia, across
the sea, we find, on the other hand, a fervid and dynamic
dramatic culture. Java, under Hindu rule from the seventh to
fourteenth century, has been fertilised artistically by varying cultures, and, like the rest of Indonesia, has absorbed new ideas
without being dominated by the successive waves of conquest.
Sundanese dance, for example, is famous, merging into true drama
in such pieces as the Tari-Topeng or mask dance, where a wife,
disguised as a prince, seeks her husband and, in hostile country
dons the " topeng " which will hide her identity still further as
she adventures among the demons who haunt the way. In
Sumatra, in a sense, we reach the happy union of all those
dramatic qualities and conventions which we have noted. The
ideal for the Sumatran dancer is to achieve perfect " gaya " or
grace, smoothness of bodily movement and expression, which
must be acquired equally by the actor. But this is a positive
thing, like the agility required by the fighter or the athlete, a

creative virility far removed from the crude force and mere weight or bodily mass encouraged in some western " physical cultures ". The finest example is the dance fight of " Penchak ". Alertness, anticipation, full harmony of personality and human

Fig. 15.—Impressions of actors in dance drama. Palace dancer at Angkor Vat (left). Festival dancer in Laos (right).

abilities, are shown in this art—which must never exert its final force, as it would on the battlefield for which it was originally intended. It is the dramatic rehearsal for actual combat.

In the palace drama of central Java, however, uninterrupted

despite external changes through a thousand years, we find utter refinement, elegance, and delicate precision, combined with the inner strength and creative purpose which mark true art. The orchestra is possibly the most developed of all those in eastern theatre; the gamelan is the melodic element, but the percussion accompaniment is an " ultimate " in variety and expressiveness; upwards of a hundred different instruments, bongs, benong, gongs, bells, xylophones, can produce the most delicate chime or the deepest drum notes. Again, singers intone the story while the drama is danced. The plots as commonly, are drawn from the Ramayans and Mahabharata, with the addition of local legend and story; the costumes and movements of the actors are in the tradition of Indian theatre, but sharpened and stylised to accord precisely with the mood of the story and the comment of the music.

The theatrical activity of Java is wide in scope. More specifically religious temple plays are still acted—" mystery " dramas such as *Tjalonarang,* the story of a witch of the eleventh century who was overcome by the priest Mpoe Bharadah. This can be heard on record " The History of Music in Sound " (His Master's Voice; Oxford University Press) as performed in Bali. The words are, however, in Kawi (old Javanese), and the orchestra contains rebab, ideophones, and percussion. The religious significance of the play survives in its powerful magic; it has (by sympathy of action) healing influence.

At furthest remove from the " total " theatre of the Javanese court plays are the solo dances of Jogjakarta, where there is an abstract timelessness of situation, a moment caught and held, without progression or resolution; yet this is true drama. Any action is " off-stage " before and after. A woman defends herself, clearly and with superb control, against a demon; a man grooms himself for the girl who will refuse his advances. In place of " solo " acting of the western kind, where often the actor gives an extract from a long play, miming the implied actions as well as he can, we have here a developed dramatic form, a music-drama for the soloist, with precise and stylised dance movements to present it.

Nearer to our ideas of theatre are the Sandiwara troupes, who present comedies with music on an improvised stage; comedies, since they have the social comment and relevance which typifies that form; here you may see the original of Gogol's *Govern-*

ment Inspector, for Java knew all about the sophistications of the
civil service while European bureaucracy was still in the making;
the busy-body, who gives himself out to be some great one, fools
all the sycophantic locals, much in the style of the men with
" paint sleeves " lamented by the shepherd in the English Wakefield mystery. The stage is set up where the company acts. When
drama leaves the setting of court or temple, it builds its theatre,
its platform and shelter of plaited mats, where its audience may
gather.

Puppetry, throughout Indonesia, has always been important,
not merely as pure entertainment, but also because it is true
theatre, originating in, and reflecting its vision back to, the life
of the people. The puppeteer is himself a teacher and enlight-
ener, bringing to the people the Buddhist ideals through the
events his puppets portray. Not that there is conscious propaganda (that of course puppets can excellently present, just as
they are used for classroom teaching of specific subjects in the
west) but rather the mediation of aspects of life, thoughts that
sustain mankind, and the Indonesian approach to these. The
conflict between good and evil is shown. If the sceptic says
" What is good, and what is evil?" we have in the puppet plays
an answer; the good is the refined, the thoughtful, the sensitive,
the considerate; the evil is the coarse, careless, clumsy, thought-
less; there is the contrast between human qualities, human
strength, human faith, and mere brutality, force and stupidity.

The Wayang Kulit are large leather puppets, clad in Javanese
court costume, the popular equivalent of such drama; Wayang
Gulek, doll puppets, are not found frequently nowadays. But
there are also, and quite commonly, the Wayang Wong, human
puppets, where live actors perform in puppet convention old
Indian stories which the narrator tells. Other theatrical activities,
films, and the modern drama groups which imitate, or seek to
incorporate, elements of western theatre, also exist. The modern
theatre movement correctly assessed the essence of naturalism by
the name it chose : " Maya "—" illusion ".

Bali is unique. The Mohammedan influence stopped short before it, and Bali thus possesses to the full traditions and cultural
practices partly lost elsewhere. But so balanced is its life, so
harmonious the relationship developed without distracting conflict between social necessity and individual fulfilment, that here
we have an almost perfect combination of past achievements

with an amazing creativity which results in new art forms—enjoyed, rejected, absorbed—so that within our own lifetime experiments have started, reached their aim, and have then been re-

Fig. 16.—Balinese clowns and comedian.

turned to the general activities from which they rose. Bali presents, some would say, in its full life and individual development
a complete demonstration of the irrelevance of natural science

(as the term is understood in the west) to human living, except
(and it *is* a big " except ") as a means for securing a basis, and
establishing conditions, in which true artistry, craftsmanship,
and the fulfilment of all human powers, may be fully achieved.

In Bali we see the complex and harmonious development of
humanity, socially and individually; villages in which every person has his own happiness in contributing to the common
pleasure through painting, woodcarving, music, dance and
drama; a land where the artist is willing to go on learning
throughout life in humility and contentment; a land where
antiquity is without meaning in itself, valuable only as it has
life to contribute to the present and future; a land where imaginative life is rhythmically fulfilled in festival and ritual; where a
successful pattern has been established which leaves the individual free to achieve and society is firmly yet flexibly organised for
creation, so that it is the imperative of *living* that rules, not the
imperative of *control*. Life is, in effect, its own dictator and
shaper.

Dances of varying kinds are found, from the trance dances of
Kayukapas, where " fire walking " (which has been filmed)
baffles the onlooker, to the developed choreography of religious
and festival presentations. For to the Balinese, man in art,
drama and music, speaks to the Gods, or (if you will) extends his
own powers and perceptions to the uttermost, and at the same
time weaves round his habitation a protective spell, or (to para-
phrase again) establishes creative qualities, preserves and revivi-
fies the sources of human existence, so that they will endure,
even against the intrusion of barbarism from contemporary
western sources. In most villages the Rangda-Barong masks are
stored for use in dance ritual. Rangda is the wife of Siva,
destructive, though destructive only to create new; Barong is a
demon, but outward appearance belies his real benevolence. The
dances show the victory of life over death, the apparent fear
which will, if the villagers are brave, be swallowed up by victory
and new life. All dance is activated by, flows from, daily life.
There is no such thing as " movement " for its own sake; it is
involved in motivated action. So the Balinese will tell you that
as they work, so they walk; their bodily abilities flow from the
tasks they achieve; as they walk and move, so they dance. The
complete harmony of the dance group, the sixth sense which
enables each to move as an individual, and yet with harmonious

reference to all the others, has developed from their communal work in which all tasks are calmly shared and everyone knows his particular responsibility.

As we should expect, Bali possesses a highly organised form of theatre, Arja, based on the traditions derived from Hindu culture, is less affected in any harmful way by later events than in some other parts of Indonesia. Performance may continue through the night. The costumes are those of classical antiquity, the characters kings and gods; the antique tongue is used, with the high pitched declamation associated with Chinese theatre. We have noted above the retention in Bali of Javanese mystery plays. The significant fact for the student of drama is that all the various elements are fused into completely satisfying presentations which have relevance (despite the apparent other worldliness of the plots) for the contemporary audience—understandably, since the western artist and writer also has been forced in modern times to resort again to abstraction, symbol and myth.

We travel 1,500 miles north to the mainland. Indo-China (Vietnam) proper will summarise for us the twin dominant influences of the vast mainland area. It looks both west to India and north to China; Indian influences come to it through Cambodia and Laos; the Chinese through Annam and Tongking. Chinese conquest and infiltration are persistent in its history, and its theatre is Chinese inspired; from the thirteenth century the Hat Boi, the classical theatre of Vietnam, has existed, comparable in most ways with the Chinese " opera ". At the start of this century the Kai Luong developed from this " classical " drama, using the same conventions but introducing " modern " music and more popular themes for the action.

To complete the circle we return to Malaya. The culture of this country in itself, and its native drama, is necessarily, from its position, Indian inspired; but a vast Chinese immigrant population means that Chinese classical theatre seems in the large cities —together with other Chinese entertainment—to monopolise drama. Yet, perhaps because of this, Malaya has preserved some of the most interesting ancient drama that is still performed, away from the cities, a theatre and drama which brings us close to origins, and yet is fully developed in itself.

The " ma-yong " is found in the old kingdom of Ligor. It is acted by a company of professionals who tour the countryside. A shed serves as the necessary " base " for the actors; while they have a shelter of palm thatch the audience, squat or stand round in front. Here in embryo is the later theatre and its conventions. Scenery is, of course, unnecessary. Masks and costumes are the

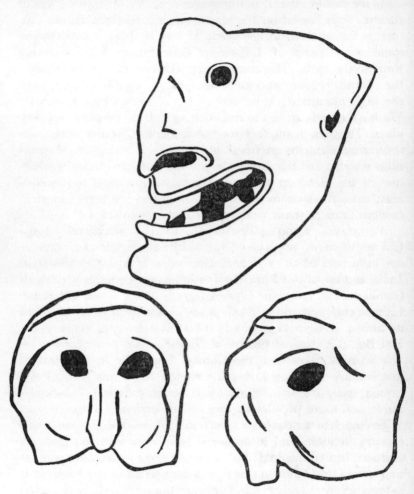

FIG. 17.—Roman theatre mask and half masks for Pulcinella in the
commedia dell'arte.

actors' only equipment, together with the orchestra of drums, gongs, and native flute. The story sections of the plot are broken (as in more elaborate eastern theatre) by interludes of singing and dancing. The stories are old romances. The prince appears with his companion, usually a clown, wearing a mask. (Compare the detailed account above of the classical *Sakuntala*). But the Malayan sense of humour usually demands that comic misadventures shall occupy the plot rather than reflective and thought-provoking events. Yet—because this performance preserves early theatre—each troupe is accompanied by a pawang or priest and the action must be prefaced by prayers to Siva, with an appeal to the local nature spirits not to be alarmed at the intrusion of forces from without. The costume is the traditional " high fashion " of the country in which the play is performed. The princess (or *ma'yong*) wears a many coloured sari, a girdle with gold buckle, silken scarf over her shoulder, the whole costume set off by gold chains, bracelets, rings, and (most typical to many western eyes) jewelled nail protectors. Her nurse played (as the eighteenth century nurse in *Romeo and Juliet*) often by a man is (again as in Shakespeare) a comic character, though more farcical.

Malaya is also associated with the shadow show or " wayang tulit ", mentioned above, which is found, not only in Java, but through the peninsula. The shed theatre is again used. The figures are cut from deer skin or cardboard and manipulated in front of a lamp so that silhouettes are thrown on a screen. The stories from the Ramayana may be performed in cycle through ten or eleven nights with some addition of local legend. Behind the curtain is the narrator; a small orchestra plays the appropriate music for each character and situation.

Finally, we may record again the adaptability and survival power of eastern drama. In a popular modern form of theatre, the " bangsawan ", the Malay has a form of drama eminently suited to his sense of comedy. Here the everyday characters of the town are satirised and burlesqued good humouredly; it is a light and contemporary form of classical theatre, relying still on romantic stories, yet presenting in these the coolies, merchants, and officials in the bustle of everyday life. It shows some similarities to gayer Edwardian musical comedy.

A last note may explain why we have left Malaya until the end. The country is largely Mohammedan, yet the theatre is Indian inspired, and its stories and conventions are those of the Hindu faith. Islam, whatever its importance to the converts in days past, has left little trace, save in the prayers before the shadow plays, a polite acknowledgment, although the real material is Hindu. We have noted above how, even when it was possible to make the recounting of Mohammed's actions a starting point for theatre in Thailand, the actual dramas quickly freed themselves from Moslem influence or content.

We shall, as we move on to consider the Middle East, discover the curious sterility of Mohammedanism in theatre. It came into lands where theatre and ritual were a normal part of life; these either ceased, or (where they endured) were a survival from pre-Mohammedan days. When folk festival still maintained dance and drama, these depended on elements tolerated and then absorbed into Islamic practice. The dignity and uncompromising simplicity of the Islamic faith seemed to antagonise and to destroy all approaches of man to God save directly; the world of the spirit, the exploration by man of nature and his own nature, were alike simplified, in the purest expression of the Faith, in obedience to the words of the Koran.

3. *The Plays*

Few written scripts are available, and perhaps the general content of the plays and their style of presentation has been sufficiently shown; moreover, the element of improvisation and variation in some popular dramatic forms really precludes detailed description. However, we may briefly glance at three types of drama. First, the Royal Khon in Thailand, now rarely performed, yet still to be seen after the last war as by Mr. Faubion Bowers from whose account in *Theatre in the East* many of the facts below are obtained. This is a kingly occasion, a ceremonial offering, which reminds us, in its general approach. of the Stuart masque, even in some details of convention. The story of one seen in recent years by Faubion Bowers was concerned, briefly, with the mission of Hanuman, the white monkey, to the underworld to rescue Rama, held there by a spell. On a high raised stage, so that as many as possible may " look in " on this rich and lavish production, the play is begun by dancers; the orchestra is on a lower platform; the costume of the ballet is familiar enough with the full sleeves and upward pointed epaulettes seen in many travel books.

Amongst the actors, however, Rama's brother (who is sending Hanuman on the mission) stands out with white face and thin red lip-line; Hanuman himself, again with whitened face and glistening white costume, is even more conspicuous. The singers announce the name of each character; then changing their style and tone, speak the lines supposed to be said by the actor, who mimes correspondingly. Music varies (and is recognised by the audience) according to each situation.

Conventionally other actors " freeze " while attention is focused on the " speaker " who alone moves. Left on stage,

Fig. 18.—Chinese shadow puppet figures.

Hanuman revels by himself in a kind of virtuoso monkey performance, not dissimilar from " Monkey " in the Chinese Opera. Then he sets out on his way to the other world, hampered by opponents, such as the magician who sends an elephant (played by two men under a cloth) against him. But Hanuman, the invincible spirit of *joie-de-vivre*, overcomes him, only to have to fight flames (agitated red streamers), and to contend with a plague of mosquitoes (again presented visually, not as in classical Indian theatre by the dance-mime of the hero). He arrives at the lotus pond, where the monster guardian of this way to the underworld, half monkey, half fish, is recognised by him as his own son (for the elemental forces are not impeded by recognised conventions of mating); to convince the guardian of his identity, however, Hanuman must work the great miracle; the magic music is played; and Hanuman, the creative demiurge, emits the moon and stars, which at once shine out in the stage setting. Then, realising that the quickest way to the underworld is down the lotus stem, Hanuman jumps, diving off the stage into the centre of the " lotus " and so reaches his goal. Court officials form the dance group which ends the performance; there is a general obeisance to the King, and his own departure. The association of courtiers with the performance, the fantasy theme which yet has its serious implications and overtones, the stage machinery, the careful emphasis on dance and music, parallel (almost surprisingly) Stuart court masques in general content and convention.

A curious blending of old and new may be witnessed in the popular presentations of the same country, the Lukhon. Dance and dialogue, dramatic event and vocal interlude, are now patterned to form a theatrical production which appeals to all tastes in the crowded audience. *Manohra,* the story of a kinnara —half bird, half woman (we, too, have *Swan Lake*)—opens on a back scene of blue sky and mountain peaks, for the kinnaras (who begin the action with a dance) live in the Himalayas. They shed their clothes (but are still decently covered) to bathe behind a gauze veil that represents the watery pool. The huntsman enters, to boast that he will capture the most beautiful as a wife for his prince. Later, we see Manohra, unhappy among mortals, although she loves the Prince who comes to take leave, since he has to go to war. The scene is embroidered with a ballet of palace girls; the prince is also played by a girl.

The ensuing battle is presented as a ballet, with entries through the audience—convention adopted by the more daring in western theatre. Then come the useful servants, who talk in colloquial Siamese, as they sweep and tidy, to give us all the news. While the Prince is away, a wicked Brahmin, to ensure that there will be no heir, so that his own nominee will be able to take the throne, has persuaded the weak king to offer up the bird-woman (a semi-divine creature) as a sacrifice to ensure the renewal of his kingly powers. Animals for the sacrifice enter. Manohra is ready for the pyre, but she begs the favour of being allowed to dance for the last time. She does so, and, of course, flies away, lifted by stage machinery to the " heavens ". The prince, on his return, pursues her to the Kinnara Palace. There Manohra is purifying herself from the taint of humanity. The prince begs the Kinnara ruler to allow him to take back his wife. Can love overcome the barriers between the worlds? His request is granted, provided that he can recognise his love as she dances with others. He knows her every movement, and is reunited with her.

A drama such as this demands a long and detailed commentary; allusions to abstruse points of ancient faith—the renewal of kingship, for example; the nature of sexual passion and the breaking down of apparently sacrosanct differences; the combination of everyday comment with the fantastic and supernatural which legitimately intrude. All combine to form a unified experience satisfying to the audience. We may compare and contrast such a western reflection in dance-drama as *The Prince of the Pagodas*. Yet the Lukhon clearly (because of the attitude of its audience) may have an immediacy and " reality " beyond that of our own ballet for us. The artistry and delicacy of the actors' movements and the beauty of dance more than compensate for any apparent crudity in setting, a crudity (in any case) which is related to western naturalism.

In the Likay we have an even more popular dramatic style, played on a platform reminiscent of the *commedia,* and, like that, without setting, save for the decorated backing which bears the name of the troupe. Here a story is dramatised from night to night, extended or amplified at the will of the company or the interest of their public. The plots are no better and no worse than the twists and turns of popular film or its predecessor, the western melodrama. So in *The Red Silk Bandit* the young man uncertain of his birth (a prince in reality), the wicked prime minister, the good queen and her daughter forced to live in the woods (the daughter in the guise of a man seeking food) and the Red Silk Bandit of the title (who turns out to be a woman) are all involved in complicated, surprising, and amusing events, not forgetting a rare element in Eastern drama, the sex-battle, for the prince (disguised) swears to marry the princess (disguised) who has struck him in anger. Consider whether some of our own (even standard) plays have schemes of action that are any more feasible. It is by the presentation the human situations, the contact with real emotions—in audience and actors—that the drama is ultimately to be evaluated.

Finally, let us recall the plot of the "musical comedy" theatre in Malaya, for it has resemblances to the new "musicals" in the west, a development in theatre which seems to bring east and west nearer. Here everyday types, the labourers, business men, rickshaw men, and the countrymen (equally popular on the stage in slightly exaggerated portrayal in the west) all enter realistically in plots which have still the basis of romantic story. *West Side Story*, for all its apparent harsh modernity, was in reality an equally romantic and legendary theme.

4. Summary

The descriptions of plays and performances outlined above have indicated the variety of methods used. The student may like to consider some recurring features in Far-Eastern theatre. (i) The unlocalised platform stage, (ii) The two forms of this— either a space in a village, backed by a temporary shelter, or the platform proper associated originally with a temple or shrine, (iii) The resultant quick movement from "scene" to "scene", (iv) The close association of dance with all dramatic forms, and, equally, the persistent dramatic basis even when we move into "pure" dance, (v) The importance of music, not merely as "melodrama", but as cue, communication of mood and even indication of action (sexual intercourse, shown by the actors merely as a stroking movement of the hand, is "presented" by the music), (vi) The use—or omission—of masks, (vii) The introduction of stage machinery and/or "scenery" in two types of drama—(a) the court spectacle, (b) the popular theatre. On the other hand, in "main stream" practice, scenery is omitted and in the most developed and refined presentation is regarded as a rather "unrealistic" intrusion. "Total theatre" does not need such "props", which may prevent by their very artificiality the audience's full emotional response to situation. Naturalism emphasises that quality of "maya" which the higher forms of theatre seek to pass through and beyond.

CHAPTER VIII

THE MIDDLE EAST

1. *Historical Background and Early Drama*

In this area of the world students face a difficulty shared with those who attempt to record man's achievements here in other branches of human activity, which has been summarised by Frankfort, in the monumental *Art and Architecture of the Ancient Orient* as " lack of cultural continuity ". Mesopotamia —and Asia Minor—have been subject to wave after wave of invasion, reacting in varying ways on the culture pattern. While the whole area has been of tremendous importance, fertile in the spread of ideas, the establishment of any developed drama or dance tradition has been almost impossible. One can watch drama perhaps " in transit ", as a people move into the area, bringing certain traditions with them, and then again transmit their ideas to other peoples, either by further migration or by cultural exchange.

Finally, we must remember that here is a great land route, the bridge that links Africa, Asia, and Europe, and that in Palestine for thousands of years the armies marched and the peoples travelled. To the East and South of this narrow fertile strip lie the great deserts and the nomadic pastoralists; to the S.W., the empire of Egypt; to the north, the way to Europe and Mongolia; and to the east, the productive lands of Babylon and Assyria, modern Iraq. Again, from below the fertile Crescent came Mohammedanism, with the puritanical single-mindedness we have already noticed, just as opposed to the elaboration of artistic experience as were seventeenth century Puritans in our own country.

The early Sumerian civilisation developed round the city states of the Euphrates-Tigris valleys, contemporary with the Indus valley Harappa culture and the rise of the Nilotic communities. From the remains of those times and the great preflood grave pits at Ur of the Chaldees, there is sufficient evidence of ritual dance, and music, including the lovely harps found at Ur. Each township centred its life on the great temple; the God dominated pattern of society is as marked as in later Eastern cultures. Lutes and drums are depicted, as well as dancers.

It is as a forcing ground for later dramatic patterns that the Middle East is really notable. Here were the earliest communities which relied on agriculture for their life, the earliest sowings of emmer wheat. When a people turns to agriculture its whole behaviour relationship with environment undergoes fundamental re-adjustment. It is important that growth should succeed. Yet there is a time in the year when all vegetation seems to pause, or even to die. At that time, the whole life of man is in jeopardy. He must try by attitude and enactment to help the earth to revive. And he can do that by himself exemplifying all the primal energies of which he is capable. So arise the feastings, tumult, and noise, of the winter solstice. Then comes in Spring the joyful resurrection of the earth, recorded so lovingly in the Song of Solomon, itself a hymn of renewal and festival. And with this the trust that out of death shall come life, for the seed must be buried and apparently be condemned to death. If man can only associate himself with this new life, he may be fed. The seed dead in the earth appears again as by a miracle—the hidden forces have brought germination and the green shoots. Here, then, humanity is brought into much closer relationship, through the rhythms of the seasons, with the hidden powers of Being which work through seasonal changes; into much closer relationship, too, with the varying forms of life, and the life force itself.

So there come the Festivals of Death and Rebirth, the search for fertility and life. The cults of Adonis and Tammuz, their weeping mourners, portray in dramatic action the death and renewal of earthly life, and man's attempt to associate himself in his work powerfully with this, a true entry into all the circumstances of his environment. Emblems, symbols, sometimes animal forms, represent various aspects of the life force. (Note, in passing, that Tammuz is called the " chief goat ", an animal commonly held to represent creative energy.)

In addition to such folk festivals and the ecstatic worship of the Mother Goddess associated with Syria and Asia Minor (afterwards identified with other deities) we have the more sophisticated dancers at feasts, the court musicians, and all the pomp associated with the later Babylonian and Assyrian kingdoms following the Sumerians in the river valleys. We have also Semitic invasion of the settled lands, typically that of the " Hebrew " peoples. From the Old Testament we can gain much information on the development of dramatic forms, dance, and music, even where a nation had no recognisable bent towards theatre, only the basic experiences which might in time arrive at full dramatic expression. And, as we all know, in later times, Jewish people have shown their imaginative sensitivity in music, drama, and art; their own early culture in Palestine was, in its most striking leaders, almost as starkly puritanical as later Mohammedanism. Yet in its folk dance, its temple ritual, and its songs, inevitably dramatic in basis and theatrical in trend, there were the materials for a splendid future whether as transmitted through the Liturgical practice of the Christian Church, or through mediaeval Judaism, unadorned though synagogue worship was.

The student would do well to read the Old Testament books. Here you will find the words of a dance drama, almost as improvised on the field of battle, the Song of Deborah, primitive and simple. Here you will read accounts of stately rituals in the Temple of Solomon; here you will discover, in the psalms, songs spoken in character and situation. The very progress of the pilgrims to the temple was a dramatic ritual, a psalm of degrees placing the singers in certain situations, acknowledged in the words of their song, as they neared the Holy Place. In the Song of Solomon we have, perhaps, a semi-dramatic composition, addressed in character to the beloved, and associated with the Spring Festival of Tammuz. On the other hand, in the Book of Job we have a serious philosophical drama, in which the problem of suffering is debated between the calamity stricken Job and his Comforters, with a startling prologue, in which God and the Adversary (Satan) discuss how Job shall be tested. In long speeches, with individual particularity of utterance and viewpoint, the case is argued. Yet Job remains faithful. In effect, the drama is never resolved, for Job is restored to fortune. Yet there is a foreshadowing of the final crisis in the tragic approach to life —" Is man no more than this?"—resolved only (so far as I can tell) in one play—*King Lear*. In Job the form is dramatic, but the treatment untheatrical, talking rather than action; but in a way it anticipates the indirect presentation of events chosen by some of our younger dramatists; and the predicament, the struggle in the mind, is essential theatre. Yet it was through the fertility dances and celebrations of the winter solstice, the festivals of the dying year, the new resurrection life, that tragedy was to develop, when, from the Middle East, the worship of intruding Dionysos was added to the more dignified Olympian hierarchy of Zeus and his subordinates.

From the north came the Hittite invasions and an Empire which endured with fluctuations for many centuries, to which the modern Turk looks back with some pride, though the race was not his. The Hittites were probably an early Aryan incursion. In the great Indo-Germanic migrations we have seen how Sanskrit speakers came into India; the invasion of Persia by Aryans went on through the second millenium B.C. The Hittites were paramount in Asia Minor at about the same time, extending down into Palestine. Then came the clash with Babylonian power, the resurgence of Assyria, the last great Babylonian Empire associated with Nebuchadnezzar, and the final carrying away of the Jews, already partly driven from their homeland (with the Northern Israelitish tribes). They began to return when Persia conquered Babylon. Egypt to the south was a declining power. Alexander with his conquests swept across the Middle East, and on to India, to found an Empire, which broke up on his death into independent states in which Hellenism and the Greek language survived as a common cultural element through the Middle East.

The Roman Empire brought for a few centuries approximate stability at least for the regions of Palestine, Asia Minor, and Egypt. When the Roman Empire in the west broke before barbarian invasions, the Roman Empire of the east (Greek in speech, though holding proudly to the name and traditions of Rome) survived as a powerful and wealthy trading nation, a bridge between east and west at Byzantium, where, it was said, all the commerce of the world was channelled to pass from one continent to another. But from the south and east the new Moslem

powers attacked. Egypt and much of Palestine was lost to them
in the seventh century. Asia Minor was gradually taken over by
the Turks. Their rule, extending into Europe and threatening
Austria at the time of the Reformation, finally ceased to expand;
for centuries the life of the Middle East seemed to stagnate.

A vivid picture of the declining Turkish Empire is given by
Kinglake's account in *Eothen* of his travels through the Middle
East in the early nineteenth century. Read that book and you will
know why, in certain circumstances, Moslem countries are inimi-
cal to theatre. The dismemberment of remaining provinces after
World War I, the rise of lively new nations, Syria, Lebanon, the
Arab States, and not least the virile young country of Israel, all
these matters we know from the news day by day as this curiously
unsettled part of the world goes on making history. This brief
glance at its past may show the differences between its cultures
and those of Far Eastern lands where theatre and art have time
to develop, to become established, creating forms and conventions which, inherited, allow each generation steadily to express
its experience of life, its imaginative vitality, through varying
patterns of music, dance, and drama. Without the secure
development attained by continuity you cannot have real
theatre. You can only imitate, or attempt to graft your own
drama into an already existing tradition, to draw vitality from
an alien stock. Much theatre in these regions today is an attempt
to use the western theatre as it now exists, and to express (mis-
takenly, one would think) Arab or Persian attitudes through
western forms.

2. *Development of Drama in Turkey*

Modern Turkey, the smaller area which contains the cities
and the nation which once controlled the Ottoman Empire, is
still a region of many traditions and many races. To travel
through even a comparatively small area is to see strongly contrasting civilisations in the remains of buildings, surviving
religions, and the customs of the people. The almost violently
theatrical landscapes contain fragments of Greek cities, cave
churches, soaring mosques and minarets, tumbled remains of
civilisations which were legendary in Roman times, towering
mountains and remote uplands with long forgotten settlements.
The very variety of the country has worked against a coherent
culture, and certainly against theatre, especially when one recalls

that the earlier Christian traditions have been submerged by Mohammedanism.

It is convenient to summarise the Middle East under Turkey, for after the collapse of the Byzantine Empire, the Turks (who regarded themselves, in some sort, certainly in the sixteenth century, as the successors of the Greek Empire) possessed much of the area from Egypt round through the Holy Land and Asia Minor, as their dominion. The Byzantine Empire retained, in the fifth and sixth centuries, long after the fall of the west, the mimes and entertainers of the Roman theatre. Classical plays were no longer performed; as in the west later, religious plays of a newer faith had taken their place. Unlike the west, however, the Byzantine culture, still unbroken, associated the new themes, at least at times, with earlier classical theatre. Whereas in the west a fresh start was made from the altar within the Church, in the east some plays apparently attempted to create (within the conventions of classical Greek tragedy) a new Christian drama. The effort was typical of the Byzantine attitude towards the preservation of the past.

How far popular drama survived, in the precarious conditions of life in Asia Minor, as distinct from the one impregnable stronghold of Constantinople, so aptly used as a symbol of artistic eternity by Yeats in his *Sailing to Byzantium,* is dubious. Probably, as in the west, the puppet performer helped to keep secular drama in being. It is interesting to see how, when prohibition, control, or difficulties of organising live companies, hinder theatre, the puppet master carries on the content of drama and brings to isolated communities the performance, conventions, and music, of full theatre; to see how, too, the puppets, in more favourable times, furnish a fresh starting point for live theatre, and yet survive in their own right, for they have their own effectiveness, their own theatrical qualities. They are an integral part of all dramatic activity through which theatre survives and extends its influence and appeal; further, through them, theatre often develops its conventions and possibilities. In Turkey, drama survived largely, in the rural districts and smaller towns, through puppets, which may well escape the general ban on visual presentation associated with the ruling faith. In Turkey, too, there are recognisable parallels with the grotesque masks of the earlier classical comedy as played in the remoter Greek cities—Karugoz is the Turkish Punch. In Greece shadow puppets are still shown; supposedly they were derived from the Far East, passed through Turkey proper, and then into Greece, where the witty and vulgar Karugoz (now Greek) gets the better of all unpopular characters, from Turks to tax-collectors. It has been suggested that the *commedia dell'arte* derived from puppet

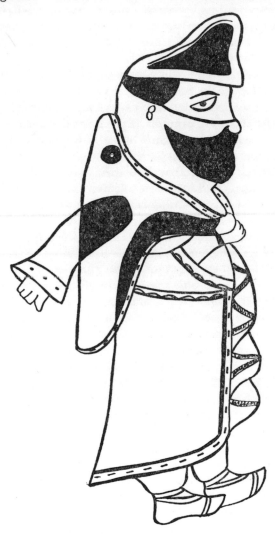

Fig. 19. Karugoz—the Turkish Punch. Shadow puppet.

figures which preserved the traditional mime characters from

Roman times to the middle ages; it might further be considered whether the sudden appearance of the *commedia* at the time of the Renaissance was linked with the fall of Byzantium and the journey to the west of so many scholars and artists. Just as puppetry preserved theatre traditions in Turkey, so perhaps this same puppetry fertilised western professional practice.

The Turks themselves appear first in written record as the Tu-Kiu, a Chinese term for the people of the region extending from Mongolia to the Black Sea. Their own writing is first found in the Orkhon inscriptions in Northern Mongolia; in their conquests they adopted the literary forms of more advanced cultures with which they had relationships as neighbours—the Arabic-Persian civilisation, for example. Epic narrative, prose memoirs, political and legal tracts, form a large part of their work, until in the mid-nineteenth century some writers adopt western forms, among these the drama, as well as the novel and the essay.

In origin the Turks and associated groups—such as the Huns—were a nomadic horse culture, patriarchal in organisation. While the western populations became Moslem, the eastern (as in more settled eastern countries) tended to superimpose new beliefs on older religious practice, such as animism. It is not to be expected that they, any more than the Germanic tribes who invaded Britain in the fifth century, should bring with them any theatre beyond simple ritual dances and festivals. We have already noted the only legitimate development of theatre in Moslem countries, the story chant which may be recited and extended by ceremonial at great Festivals. That indeed occurred also in Turkish culture. Suleiman Chelebi (died 1421) composed a life of Mohammed recited on solemn festivals; the tendency of such story presentation to develop into theatre proper is known.

Yet when in the nineteenth century drama appeared it was as a borrowing from western style theatre. There is no strong native tradition such as emerges in Jewish practice, even when obscured through periods of time. One of the most celebrated of Turkish dramatists, Abdul ak Ahmed Bey, for example, experimented freely with western styles of drama, using both prose and verse, writing plays romantic in scope and approach, yet at the same time most successfully (perhaps with reason considering the Turkish spirit and traditions) using the classical conventions of French seventeenth century drama, deriving a theme from Corneille's *Horace*.

On the other hand, there is much folk-lore and traditional custom—undeveloped though it is—in the many communities of modern Turkey, not forgetting the mixed races, the blue eyed Kurds, and other elements in the population. It has been conjectured that the purest Turkish blood is to be found (a mixture of Alpine and Mongoloid strains) in the Altai and Volga basin. Contrariwise, the minstrel songs of the life of Mohammed developed in the fourteenth century in Anatolia, as the Turks gradually subdued the Byzantine provinces.

3. *Drama in Israel*

Now that the Jewish race has a national home, its natural sensitivity and artistic impulses find expression in interesting and varied ways. In Israel amateur groups have maintained, or developed, traditional dances and festival rituals belonging to many different Jewish communities such as those scattered and almost isolated for centuries in various out of the way parts of the Middle East, or, on the other hand, brought by new immigrants from the west who have theatrical experience based, not only on modern western theatre, but also on their own development of folk drama. Notable here are the mediaeval Purim plays. The festival of Purim in early March commemorates the events told in the Book of Esther. A semi-religious observance, all kinds of amusement were associated with it in the later Middle Ages; it seems likely, according to some authorities, that the observance owes something to Persian influence.

Masquerades in which actors impersonated the characters in the story were opposed by many Jewish religious authorities, for the plays themselves were probably suggested by carnival mummings of the non-Jewish population. Indeed, the comic rabbis, citizens, and devils, who were introduced in performance, the improvised dialogue and by-play, were certainly not wholly acceptable to Jews or apparently helpful to their traditions and faith. Yet the theme—typically—of a struggle against overwhelming odds (which led to other stories than that associated with the feast being used) and the final chorus foretelling Israel's salvation, was basically healthy and dramatically appealing. Joseph, David and Goliath, Moses, all at times figured as the central characters. Plays were performed wherever possible—barns, houses, even workshops. When in the seventeenth century they began to acquire a more polished and settled script they approximated still nearer to contemporary Gentile drama; the *commedia* was drawn upon and stock figures there became in effect also the characters of the Purim play—the Braggart Captain clearly was Goliath, Harlequin was the adversary Satan, and so on.

In the eighteenth century (possibly not without thought of the serious presentation of Biblical themes staged by ordinary theatre —the English Biblical plays of the Elizabethan period come to mind) attempts to provide a worthy script, free from irrelevancies, led to the presentation at Prague of a revised and purified Esther play. The Haskala groups continued careful and thoughtful production of Purim plays, but gradually the scope of their drama was extended. Permanent Yiddish theatres were here and there established. Yet the early history of modern Israeli theatre owes much to the Purim plays which released the national genius for mimetic expression, and so helped the present versatile theatre of Israel. As in England modern theatre can look back to the Easter trope, so the Israeli may consider the rough energy of the early Purim plays as part of his heritage. One must note that according to some authorities mimicry may have had a place in Jewish festivals (mainly the Purim) from early times; but this is not proved. (Landau : *Studies in Arab Theatre and Cinema*, p. 2.)

4. *Plays in the Middle East*

The use by Turkish and Arabian story-tellers of mimicry—during which they change their head-dress and imitate the movements and gestures of their characters—is an interesting parallel with the wearing of different masks by Thespis in the early Greek theatre. Curiously, too, it bears out Brecht's statements on the characterisation which results from story telling, and supports some of his typical ideas on the actor's work. Mimicry of this kind is one element, at least, in the theatrical presentation. That these imitations could develop into drama proper is indicated by travellers' records. Thus, in 1874-75 Warner saw Egyptian sailors performing (on a Nile pleasure boat) a rough play in which they imitated various dignitaries and officials, bribing and receiving bribes. It was little more than a charade, yet acute in observation and successful as a simple farce.

More developed plays (apparently surviving in villages from a much earlier time) were seen by E. W. Lane, who described one such in the earlier years of the nineteenth century. In this a poor fellah is in debt; he is beaten, and is released only after his wife has bribed a Coptic clerk (disliked by the Muslims) with food, a village chief with money, and the district governor with her body. But plays seem to have been more usual in Egypt, despite Moslem occupation, than in other " Arab " countries. Belzoni saw two plays in 1815 after a wedding ceremony, plays which clearly had a long ancestry in folk tradition. First came dancing, and then, suitably, full drama; a traveller to Mecca wants to buy a camel. He is cheated—since the go-between charges him one price, and gives less to the actual owner of the camel. At length the camel appears (two men covered with a cloth). The would-be pilgrim objects—it is such a bad camel. Then the seller turns up and finds it is not the camel he sold. So the go-between is guilty of a double deception—he has substituted an inferior camel for the one sold and has claimed too much money. He is beaten and runs off. A little farce followed, in which a European was the butt and the clown. This important visitor from abroad comes to the house of a poor Arab, who wishes to appear wealthy and orders a sheep to be killed. His wife reports that the flock has strayed—and it would take too long to go after them. " Kill four fowls," says the Arab. Alas, they can't be caught; so two pigeons must be obtained—but these are not to be found. So in the end the traveller has sour milk and coarse bread.

As noted above, some religious festivals have in them the possibilities of drama, and in Persia, where Mohammedanism is superimposed on earlier belief and practice, results are almost terrifying. The so-called Passion Play—the Ta' ziya presented there during the first ten days of the month of Muharram—shows the killing of Hasan, Husain, and other members of Ali's family in the eighth century. This slaughter of the members of the prophet's family by the new rulers had lasting effects in the Muslim community. But the curious trend in drama to build round— sometimes almost without relevance—a central theme is here shown in other events from Old Testament and folk-lore which furnish additional episodes. Whether or not these were intended to lessen the tension and to spread the emotion safely through a period of time, as some authorities suggest, audience feeling is often so stirred that in past times (and perhaps even now) spectators would vent their excitement on any passing non-Muslim foreigners. This is audience participation—with a vengeance!

Actors also, grief stricken and completely identifying themselves with the actions they present, have on occasion committed suicide. Performances take place in the open air or indoors, sometimes in actual theatres, but more normally in the precincts of a mosque.

Between the wars, authority restrained the plays, though they have a vitality and appeal which seems likely to ensure survival. Stage effects are lavish but crude—the gory head on a pole, the real blood, the real horses—yet heightened emotions accept at the same time the apparently miraculous. Music accompanies, women's parts are played by men, and animals (other than horses) are portrayed by human actors. Acting is loud, declamatory, and exaggerated, but the whole effect is convincing, so much so that (as we have seen) theatrical illusion ceases and real death and horror supervene.

From this " dramatic prototype " other plays have apparently been derived. Versions of the " Passion Play " were known also in Arabic and Turkish. On the whole, however, one feels that theatre as such, until modern times, was not encouraged in Moslem countries; and, as some have said, the Passion Play may be in essence Zoroastrian however converted by its association with Mohammedan events into a Moslem religious rite. Perhaps this, too, is the explanation of its violent effect. For devout Mohammedans it is either actuality or nothing. So the dramatic presentation becomes a religious instigation to immediate action in real life.

5. *The Theatre of the Shadow Plays*

Only in the obviously " pretend " shadow plays has the Middle East a lasting dramatic tradition. This, as Landau states is " the most important fore-runner of the theatre " in the Middle East. (op. cit. p. 9.) It appeals to all classes; it expresses faith, fable, farce, and romance. It is uncompromisingly theatrical.

Landau thinks it is possible that Turkish conquerors retained the services of Byzantine actors. Further, the commercial ties between Turkey and Venice (and Italy generally) might encourage exchange of ideas. In any case, the type characters of Turkish shadow puppets are a parallel development to those in the late Roman mime and the renascent *commedia dell'arte*. Two central characters are Hagivad and Karugoz, who follow various trades and meet all the people whom the playwright (or puppet master) desires to introduce—in total a rich portrayal of life—merchants, watchmen, boatmen, moneylenders, policemen, drug addicts, paupers, hunchbacks, debauchees, stutterers, acrobats, and foreigners. Clearly no persons of worth may be presented; Sultans, high officials, and respectable women, are absent. Women who do appear are mainly negresses, witches, prostitutes, or entertainers. Music accompanies action, and a suitable theme may introduce and signify a character, especially a foreigner. Satiric intent, aimed at pretenders or swindlers, was never far away. Karugoz, the Turkish " Punch ", knew that he was a fool, and, while exposing the folly of others, could laugh at himself. So he looks for a job, guided by Hagivad and shows his incompetence; or he tries to do forbidden things, from illicit desire or stupid curiosity, and is caught by the police. But the Turkish shadow play introduced also stories from Persian sources and the Arabian Nights. Its popularity endured almost to our own times, but is now superseded by entertainments and theatrical forms of western origin. Clearly, however, the traditions and attitudes of Karugoz must remain as a force in Turkish humour and performance.

In Egypt the shadow play, in a cultured community, with cosmopolitan background, wealth, and artistic taste, became a recognised dramatic form, for which such a learned physician as Muhammad ibn Daniyal wrote plays which survive perpetuating the manners and society of Egypt in his time (1248-1311). These plays are in poetry and versified prose, completed (as stage compositions) by instructions and advice on presentation. Theatrical reliance for acceptance on a religious sanction is exemplified in the apparently stereotyped prologue; prayers are offered on behalf of the ruler and God and His Prophet are praised. The second play of his trilogy treats of two rogues, one a shrewd but shiftless traveller, the other a wandering preacher with most unorthodox and amusingly irregular views. Their journey, with the people they meet in market and town, exhibits a whole gallery of contemporary people to the audience, snake-charmers, quack doctor, an epileptic boy, animal tamers, acrobats, a sword swallower, and many others, each of whom tells his trade and shows his work.

The relationship between this sophisticated (and internationally famous) Egyptian shadow theatre and the apparently less developed Turkish performances has been questioned. When

Selim I conquered Egypt in the sixteenth century, he was so impressed by the Egyptian shadow plays that he took six hundred performers with him back to Istanbul. This was perhaps the first really significant contact between the two " theatres ". Yet it is difficult to imagine, from the widespread performance of shadow plays, in Syria, Algeria, and other Arab speaking countries, that developments were isolated. In particular, the Turkish Karugoz, in some form or other, appears in almost all as a dominant character.

The theatre is simple. A large sheet of white linen was set up outside, or in a house, on a festival occasion, and lit from behind. The figures, cut carefully and partly transparent, with leather as the main fabric, measured from one to two feet or more in height, and were moved by the puppet master and manager by sticks which fitted into holes in their body and limbs. Assistants moved others or read the parts. Unnecessary holes were sometimes added to satisfy the Muslim antipathy to actual figures; extra mutilation guaranteed their lifelessness. (This, of course, illustrates the general opposition to stage presentation in Muslim countries.) The words could be sung or recited. The orchestra (in Egypt) might contain tambourine, drum, and oboe. In Turkey string instruments were on occasion used with the tambourine. Shadow theatre survived in Egypt even after the closure (by authority at the start of the twentieth century) of two existing theatres. Players went on tour to cafés or markets. Some scripts seem to link us with the earliest Egyptian rituals we know, in the far off days when the pyramids were built. Such is the Ship Play. The music is quiet, almost soothing. Then comes the arrival of the ship with its captain and oarsmen. We have the entry of the passengers who are to travel on the ship; the fun derives from their characterisation. The Crocodile Play, even more, typifies the life of the dwellers near the Nile. A fellah when fishing falls in, is swallowed by a crocodile, and calls for help. The fun is produced by the gibes of the real fishermen at the " amateur " fellah. However, in the end he is rescued.

One must not omit to mention a play in which a Moslem triumph over the Christian is celebrated. In the *Cloister Play* a Coptic " monk " sends his daughter time after time to rob a Moslem trader's wares. By her wiles she escapes on many occasions but is eventually caught, repents, becomes herself a convert to Islam, and marries the trader. Here is a very coherent plot; so often in the shadow plays the fun of the individual puppets constitutes the sole appeal, to the detriment of the story. In Syria and Tunisia, however, the plots are well worked and contain a valuable store of dramatic material. Karugoz figures largely and there is specific reference to his relations with the god of fertility (an inheritance from the Greek phallic comedies, so authorities state) in an Algerian play of the early nineteenth century. The use of puppets to express local political feeling intrudes; Karugoz attacks the French soldiers who come against him by beating them with the god of fertility who serves him as a stick. In 1843 the French forbade shadow plays!

6. *Theatre Today*

During the nineteenth century the theatre in the Middle East began to copy western models. France and Italy often taught the new playwrights. Beirut and Alexandria were ports open to European traders; the Italian Opera House and theatre in the latter, and French influence in the former, helped future development. Christians, were, of course, more easily led into theatre work than Moslems. Through the east there are many Christian communities, far older than the settlements of their Moslem conquerors. The first actresses were nearly always Christian or (sometimes) Jewish. The "modern" Arab theatre in Syria was established by Naqqash (1817-1855). He presented his own adaptation of Molière's *L'Avare* on an improvised stage in his house in Beirut in 1848. The compromise needed to secure better acceptance in Syria is interesting. Naqqash himself was a Maronite Christian. His methods typified the general trends in establishing Arab theatre. Names were altered to Arabic; the place of action also was altered. Comedy was written in to suit local taste. Music was added—thus bringing the play nearer in a sense to the "total" theatre of countries further east; an attempt was made to fit the music to the theme and events of the play. Men took the women's parts. All actors were at first members of his own family. Later, he built a theatre (or hall to be used for performances) near to his house. Other adaptations from, and plays similar to, those of Molière followed. In Egypt Abbas II sent Abyad, by birth a Syrian Christian, to study dramatic art in France. On his return in 1910 he formed his own troupe and presented plays in the classical French tradition, later developing other forms of drama.

7. Summary

For the present development and state of the theatre in Egypt
and other Arab countries we must refer those interested to
Landau's book. Largely, however, this development has little
more to offer us, since basically it is inspired by familiar western
forms. There is, however, in Egyptian popular theatre a demon-
strable continuity with popular farces and burlesques of native
tradition, now blended with western farce and popular entertainment. Further, as Landau implies, the new Arab theatre and
cinema have qualities which are distinctive and utilise their
racial inheritance. In this we may see a way for newer nations of
Africa, who are adopting western culture patterns, and yet increasingly conscious of their own native qualities and genius. A
mature theatre may result from the use of western theatre
and its conventions if they strive to express in and through it
their own art forms, dance, music, and particular approach to
life.

CHAPTER IX

WESTERN THEATRE

1. *Historical background*

The spread of the Indo-European races, noted first in India, continued with successive waves of migration into what is now Europe, down into Greece and the Greek islands, first merging with and then later dominating earlier Minoan and Mycenean cultures; across, into Italy, to supplant the Etruscan and similar groupings; and then from the " storm centre " of central Europe in expanding pressures which we link vaguely in our minds with the Gaelic and Celtic peoples, Saxons and Angles, Danes, Norman invaders—intermarrying, first, with earlier non-Aryan races, and later with the preceding Indo-European population. Here and there, as in, perhaps, remoter valleys of Wales and Andorra, pockets of earlier peoples survived. In the main, however, by assimilation and intermarriage they were incorporated. Similarly, Indo-Europeans moved into Russia, with admixture of Turkish blood in the south-eastern parts, or, as with the Finns, the intermingling of other non-Aryan groups. But the main westward movement was not finished. In the fifteenth century, the quest continued. Indo-Europeans from various countries in Europe moved into the Americas, and in succeeding centuries into other parts of the world, either to occupy almost uninhabited areas, as in Australia, or to influence the already established cultures of older races.

Since most of these invaders and settlers had a more developed civilisation, there was a tendency (now happily weakening) for the inhabitants of such countries to ape cultural patterns and art forms of the Indo-Europeans. Thus the present theatre of the Americas and of Australia is necessarily that of the western world, since the newcomers brought with them a developed theatre, or remained sufficiently in contact with their countries of origin to share and to import contemporary trends in western theatre.

The native theatre of Africa (except as noted above) and the Americas remains in the pre-theatrical form of dance-drama and festival. Rarely has it emerged into full theatre, though the student should be prepared to meet exceptions to this rule. Further—and this is significant for the future—in Central and South America, through the centuries of Spanish rule, the influence of the native races has produced a synthesis of dance and festival which reflects many completely un-European approaches, just as in the dominant Catholic religion acceptable beliefs and practices have been assimilated (without disturbing essential Christian faith) from earlier native cults.

Let us also remember that the invading Indo-Europeans were themselves of mixed race, and that the dance traditions and folk drama, say, of Spain have their own distinct quality. My attention has been directed by Mr. John Edmonds to such a festival in Mexico, where a nominally religious procession is accompanied by drumming and chant of native origin performed by the spectators who line the street. Although, in a sense, we must class the practising theatre in such a country as " western ", yet with a new sense of nationality, a pride in past folk culture and art, the Mexican theatre of the future will have much that will differentiate it from the general western tradition, if indeed it does not, as seems likely in some " new " countries, establish theatrical patterns which show a fresh synthesis of music, dance, and mime, perhaps akin to eastern theatre. Certainly the gorgeous costumes and décor of traditional dance derived from Aztec culture would encourage such a theatre; on the other hand, it may be that drama proper will keep aloof from dance and music.

In the United States there has been varied theatrical practice and much conscious experiment and thought. Educationally, at the university level, the United States has given much time and money to drama, with professorships, schools of playwriting, experimental theatres, and community playhouses. Yet—paradoxically—America is associated in most people's minds with the establishment and expansion of one form of theatre, the motion picture, which, again, has (as is the custom among the Indo-

Europeans) thrown roots back to the lands from which the " Americans " came, the mainland of Europe, so that now each country there has an important film making industry; and (finally) this form of theatre has been accepted and used by countries of the east, mercifully often within the framework of their existing dramatic approaches and conventions, and not entirely in accordance with the naturalistic nineteenth century basis of western film. Some Chinese " opera " films thus preserve a wider approach to theatre. Anything which persistently and of set purpose narrows the artistic scope and appeal of theatre—in film or otherwise—is surely not, in principle, a good thing.

Without recapitulating in detail the troubled history of the western world we can distinguish three formative influences (a) the Greek, (b) the Roman Empire and its established and settled rule—a rule and tradition that has survived in many western institutions, legal and cultural, to the present day, (c) the influence of the Christian Church, its rituals, and its approach to the " life forces ", the " tragic " bases of existence. It will be seen at once that two of these powers (at least) were in part not Indo-European in origin. Greek theatrical culture stemmed very largely from Athens, where invaders had intermarried with earlier inhabitants (contrast the Spartan isolation of conquerors from their originally more cultured subjects), and where the drama was founded on the Dionysiac cult, itself from the east, a worship akin in impulse to the mourning for Tammuz. Dionysos was a late-comer, even an intruder, among the Olympian Gods. As for Christianity it was rooted in the developing God-awareness of the Jewish race, in association perhaps with other human approaches and insights through the ages; the contribution from the west to its essential " Christ doctrine " was negligible in the first instance, although the Greek power of philosophic and theological discussion and the Roman ability to organise gave the religion its mental, spiritual, and physical, sinews in the world. We shall note the development of drama, first in Greece, then in Rome, and finally in the various countries which, at first, provinces of the Roman Empire, or independent tribal groupings, gradually patterned themselves to make modern Europe. At the same time we shall recognise (as we have already recorded) that each of these countries and cultures had its own existing folk drama and ritual based on pagan beliefs just as did all other nations of the world. These earlier, non-Greek, non-Roman, non-Christian, patterns survive, sometimes in folk-dramas and dances, always in child play, often breaking through into present-day theatre.

2.   *Development of Drama*

The worship of Dionysos, associated both with the local celebration of the winter solstice, and more typically with the spring-time festival, those two significant times in the agricultural calendar, furnishes the generally recognised basis of Athenian drama, which, emerging into theatre, overshadowed and later absorbed any other local traditions and observances. Dramatic rituals in the mystery cults—as for example at Eleusis—are referred to, sometimes in existing plays. The important developments by which dramatic enactment becomes theatre, however, depend on Dionysos.

From songs in honour of the god, recited to a chorus which danced and chanted in response, the followers of the god, we move, traditionally through Thespis, to impersonation of characters in the story by the soloist who dons various masks as he presents the different persons. (Students may like to compare, at a far remove, the mediaeval ballads, where, in early versions, the words of the speakers are given without any " he said ", " she said ", a vivid immediacy of statement connecting the form with drama, so that children can act almost at once the story presented. Here, too, is the " chorus " refrain, often almost meaningless now, and the nearness of dance, for " ballad " and " ballet " are related words.) Once the soloist impersonates the characters we have " drama "; with additional watching worshippers, independent of the chorus in the large community, we have the start of " theatre ", a " showing ", as well as " drama ", the " doing ".

There were two differing presentations. First, there was the solemn enactment outside the temple itself; compare early Shinto drama in Japan. Second, there were performances given by touring bands of devotees in other localities. In both cases the approach was serious, whatever excitement might be generated. Here is " tragedy " concerned with the great questions of man's destiny, life, death, birth, struggle, hate; love, the elemental and ultimate things, the questions of fate and personal responsibility.

In addition, there were local village festivities, which, however associated with Dionysos, had a somewhat different impulse. The laws and totems which bind a primitive community are, for survival purposes, necessarily stringent; moreover, as time goes on the accumulated weight of custom and taboo becomes almost intolerable. Such communities need, if they are to remain healthy, periodic times of comparative licence, in which, for a while, inhibitions are thrown off and the life forces flow freely. Such festivals as the Saturnalia, the Boy Bishop, All Fools, and the Lord of Misrule, remaining in more sophisticated western culture, witness to this amply. Clearly, too, such times will fit well in northern climes with the mid-winter " stirring up ", the evocation of the life force and its energising powers. So even to-day our " Christmas " is in reality such a time of feasting, drinking, and (chastely now with the mistletoe) of sexual freedom, Yuletide, in fact, although fittingly associated with the new life of the Christ child as man, has moved to a higher religious perception. Even more important, such a time allows social re-adjustment, only a little at a time, maybe, but liberty gives scope for the suggestion (in uninhibited actions) of better ways and demonstrates the uselessness of some taboos. Again, free speech is allowed; there can be frank criticism under the aegis of the festival (or the god) of those in authority; jest may contain the sting of truth. So avails the licence of the Fool, the Boy Bishop, or the frank exchange of *badinage* and scandal at the village festival.

Here are the springs of comedy. This does not aim at the ultimate and serious bases of life, but at those which press harder, because closer—social tensions, the efforts to adjust happily within the community. Comedy presents and assesses in the festive period that life which flows in social activity, marrying and giving in marriage, class distinctions, snobberies, laughs at the eccentric, unmasks the greedy trader or the clumsy workman. Here is not the tragedy, the goat song, but the *comos* (revel) and its *ode,* the chant and song of the community, the village. So at Athens it was some time before comedy, stemming from carnival processions, free comment, and the ribaldry of village celebrations, was admitted to a place in dramatic festivals. When it did it brought two choruses, representing perhaps the procession (with the car of Thespis) that moved through the streets and the spectators who lined the sides and shouted and chanted in reply. (See above for similar developments in Ceylon and Mexico.)

In the fifth century B.C. the great dramatic festivals of Athens were established in a thriving community which prized itself on its achievements and its thought, which we have in many ways not surpassed. In tragedy the Greeks presented in action ultimate questions about man and his environment. In comedy they gibed, too fiercely as it proved, at rulers and contemporary events. When Aeschylus added a second actor, the chorus became less important. Now there was the possibility of speech from person to person on the stage. The audience's gaze and attention ignored the waiting chorus between them and the actors. When Sophocles adds a third actor to the stage, then we feel we have theatre as we know it, in embryo at least. Yet the classical Greek theatre depended largely for its effect on the songs and dances presented by the *choros*. These were an attraction in themselves, and must be made so in modern presentation, informing the audience, securing the mood of the play. Essentially the chorus is the ideal audience, responding, impersonating, and answering for, the worshippers.

As the body of worshippers becomes larger, so the chorus represents also the other devotees present, and mediates *the play* to *them* and their *response* to the " actors ". Ideally both chorus and audience are also actors. That " the audience makes its own show " is still stage wisdom. The great tragic writers show a developing and changing response to life, Aeschylus, pious yet questing, soldier and patriot, noting the power of heredity and the disaster which attends man when he " gets above himself " or " dares " the universe and, victim of *hubris*, places himself above the natural order; Sophocles, an artist in stage situation, irony, and odes which hymn the glory of man; Euripides, critical, sentimental, and presenting the unpopular with vigour, considering the sufferings, not the glory, of the wars that Greeks undertook, seeing, too, the woman's viewpoint, and challenging, by implication, the gods themselves.

Of the comedy of Aristophanes, one can only repeat that no such savage and hilarious attacks on social events and conditions have been known since his day. Politicians, personalities, cults and philosophers, are held to scorn in their actual presence, for the Attic drama was a community occasion and still a religious festival which all attended. He found that not even the protection of the god could keep him from prison; in his later comedy he moved to more general criticism in place of the fiercely personal utterances of *The Frogs.*

As we shall see, the importance of the chorus, threatened immediately dialogue took place on the stage, decreased rapidly, until in the comedy of Menander there is only formal use almost unlinked with the events of the play. Yet there were still interludes and perhaps " variety turns " between acts. In tragedy also, even by the time of Euripides, the chorus is hardly felt as an intervening force. It comments but it is not necessarily involved in the drama, as were the Elders of Argos in the *Agamemnon* of Aeschylus. In Menander's later comedy we have moved to the comedy of manners. No longer is satire personal; it is general and aimed at certain accepted social types within an equally accepted stratum of the community. We are now not so far in spirit from Molière. True, the masks are still in use—but so they were in the *commedia* from which Molière drew his early experience and material.

3. *The Early Theatre*

This developed, often, from performances before the temple. At Athens, the space between this and the intervening hill slope was the " orchestra ", the dancing place of the *choros.* The temple itself was a background; the hill-slope was the auditorium. Then, in order to secure a better surface for the dancers and their movements, the bottom of the hill was cut away and the soil thus obtained spread out towards the temple so that in place of a slope continuing to the temple there was now a level " orchestra ". The slope of the hill, by removal of soil, had become steeper, and the raising of the soil near the temple to secure a level expanse left a sharp drop between the temple and the end of the dancing space. This drop was used dramatically by Aeschylus in his early play, *Prometheus;* and the natural setting suggested his chosen locality—a desert place.

Soon, for the actors, now two in number, a small shed was erected in place, so to speak, of an earlier temple refuge. Two actors suggest two doors, an unsymmetrical arrangement, since one door must open more ceremonially for the main actor, or protagonist. Soon, therefore, it seems the three door arrangement was established. The main central door was that associated with the chief character. Further, a small platform, now that actors spoke to each other, and not merely to the chorus, ran before the little wooden shed, or *skene.* The actors were at such pains, in the vast open air setting, to raise themselves by padding, high head-dresses and stilted shoes, that it would have been stupid not to utilise the necessary speaking place in front of the *skene* (the *logeion*) as a further means of elevation, even though they were still too closely linked to the chorus to permit of further removal by a very high platform. Stone foundations of the fourth century indicate a fairly large *skene* extended across one end of the orchestra. Again, from the top of the *skene* gods could descend to earth; so the roof was the talking place of divinities—the *theologeion*. Other devices were the *ekkuklema,* on which corpses were wheeled out onto the platform before the large central door (this fact, in itself, indicates some kind of solid and level staging) the *periaktos,* three flats joined together at the edges on which simple scenic devices could be painted, turned so that each flat faced the audience as required, and machines for thunder and other effects.

A striking characteristic of the Classical Greek theatre would be massive dignity and slow movement, coupled with the hieratic gesture of the main actors, contrasting with the easier and more graceful dance movements of the *choros*. The padding of costumes, the sheer weight of masks, the need to keep the head erect because of this weight, (those who have worn modern reconstructions of classical masks will know what I mean! See also under " Ceylon " above) slowed the movements to a dignity which accorded well with the greatness of the theme and the vast expanse containing the listening and watching crowd. Acoustics were not a main problem. Seats, by the late fifth century, were no longer the grassy hill slopes but probably a nearly complete circle of stone terraces. You can, even today, test the possibilities of open air speech in the still Mediterranean air. Modern man has tended to lose the normal powers of the human voice. It is quite easy to speak (without forcing the voice) in such a way as to send the words out over large distances. (I heard an old variety artist say, looking disgustedly at a microphone in front of him, " What am I supposed to do with this thing? Lord love yer, if I'd used this at the old Chatham Empire, they'd have flung the benches at me from the gallery." After which he discarded it, and did his act without.)

In comedy you would have noticed the fantastic costumes, animal disguises, exaggeration of bodily features, and almost ecstatically farcical events. For this theatre was, like that of the

Far East today, a theatre of mime, music, dance, colour, and gorgeous ornament—a " total theatre " which had, in addition, the keen social sense of western democracy, and, even beyond that, western man's philosophic and questioning approach to environment. In a sense we are still with the old " hunting mime ", yet now it is social contentment and justice we track, and the heights of heaven we try to reach in a metaphysical " hunt ". It is still man and his environment, man and his way to life—in the highest sense—that occupies theatre.

4. *Hellenistic Theatre*

Greek influence spread over the near Middle East, following the conquests of Alexander, quite apart from the Greek colonies which already existed both there and to the west also, in Italy and beyond. Where the Greeks went, their culture inevitably spread, even when, as in Judaea, there was local antipathy. And with them went their theatrical practice by now to some extent secularised. True, (as nearly always with theatre, even today) it was associated with holiday festivals, which depend originally on religion; some kind of religious sanction and authority lay behind it, inevitably when all art was under the patronage of appropriate gods. But it was no longer a compulsive ceremony to which all citizens must bow; something of civic occasion lingered (even as in this country in the little Georgian playhouse at Richmond the Mayor and the local aristocracy had their special " boxes "); again, the wealthy patron had taken the place of the Athenian *choregus* who, for the glory of the city and his own reputation, subsidised the performance of a particular poet. But now it was essentially an entertainment, not devoid of social and religious relevance, but no longer a necessary duty. Theatres were smaller. Moreover, the functions of the chorus had almost disappeared. Intimate relationship between " orchestra " and stage was unnecessary. Inevitably, the stage was then raised higher so that actors could occupy the theatre at least on equal terms with the majority of spectators. Since the stage was higher, it was supported on pillars in place of simple stone foundations, and actors were poised ten feet in the air, with the three formal doors of entrance behind them. (This has been unnecessary discussion on this matter; but the architectural facts are plain; and illustrations show the use of the raised stage.)

Where there were no permanent theatres, in the less populous

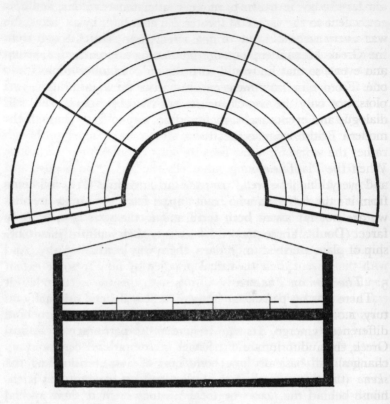

Fig. 20.—Sketch plan of Greco-Roman theatre. (Termessos).

western regions, local mimes, using the stock masks of the type characters, set up temporary wooden stages, sometimes, again, with access to ground level by steps. These performed in various parts of Italy and formed the earliest companies that appeared at Rome on Festivals and holidays, not greatly appreciated by the serious minded ruling class. Clearly, there was influence from Greek theatre; the earliest Italian plays draw on Greek models, rough local types in comedy being gradually "sophisticated" in more urbane Greek themes. Basically they were probably similar in origin. Bands of players, now semi-professional, went from place to place to serve the holiday crowd, yet possessed a trade of their own, if need be, in addition to their work as actors. Sometimes they were known by the type they presented in their plays. Plautus may illustrate these points. His second name Maccus indicates one of the clown parts in Roman comedy; this, again, is equivalent to the Greek Macco in the country Phylax plays. He was a very successful playwright, often using themes drawn from the Greek Menander; but the Roman audience needed action and event, so that he would on occasion combine two plots into one. From him later western dramatists drew inspiration and plots, not only the neo-classicists, but Shakespeare as well. His dialogue and events are easily accepted; some " gag " lines of the modern British stage came down almost unchanged (although rather the worse for wear because out of context) from Plautus. When the Plautine young man tells the girl, " Be a *good* girl and everything'll be well," and the girl answers, " Where I come from it's the *bad* girls who have all the fun," we are aware that we are not far away from fertility pre-occupations in modern farce. (Doubts are expressed by some scholars as to the authorship of plays ascribed to him and the events of his life.)

5. *The Roman Theatre*

There was no permanent theatre at Rome until the first century B.C. When Romans did engage in theatre construction, differences emerge. In the Hellenistic theatre, as in classical Greek, the auditorium and the stage quarters were (despite many changes) still basically two buildings—the auditorium and the *skene* (the term *proskenion* applied to the front of the scene house behind the actors or to the actual stage in front of the skene.) The Romans were concerned with building theatres in many places, often where no natural slope outside a hill top town helped construction. They faced the task of building an artificial hill of seats; to secure the firmness of structure the *skene* was extended to meet the ends of the semi-circle of seats. Now we have a single theatre building. But the almost complete *circle* of the classical Greek theatre has become a *semi-circle*; the orchestra space itself is a semi-circle bounded by the stage. Again, the prosperous communities and spreading provincial cities of the mighty Empire needed buildings able to accommodate their crowding spectators. Theatres are correspondingly large. In a sense, theatre is again a civic and imperial activity; state holidays need state entertainment for the masses. The emperor or the local authorities (often through the wealth of those elected to serve on the local council) must provide diversions. Amusement itself is a kind of social imperative, a duty and a communal ethic.

Roman theatres are, all in all, the most splendid architectural achievements that drama has produced. Even though battered by the years they are still in use in parts of the world. The original splendour of the now vastly extended scene house, stretching the whole width of the theatre, with its sculptures, three main, two subordinate (and extra), doorways, its decorated stage roof, and the *velum* or curtain that rises and sinks before actors, can be dimly imagined from existing remains and pictorial reconstruction. We have indeed come a long way from the little wooden shed of six centuries before!

6. *Roman Performances*

The great size of the theatres, the unavoidable noise of a large crowd, even in earlier days, made spoken dialogue indistinct. Moreover, the cosmopolitan nature of the audience drawn to Rome from Africa, Asia, and even barbarian immigrants from parts of the European Empire, meant that a great number of the spectators would be unable to follow speech with any ease; in the provinces local dialects and variant forms of Latin would pose similar difficulties. Basically, then, the Roman playhouse was necessarily a theatre of spectacle and mime, things seen, things performed, things danced, and (where voice seemed necessary) things sung. On occasion the stock characters of the " mimes " (see above) might perform, but their great (and lasting) popularity was in the smaller theatres or open spaces of the country districts. (Remember that " mime " is here a word for an actor in general, not necessarily one who acts without speech.)

In large city theatres, variety shows of various kinds were popular, tumblers, acrobats, dancers, performing animals, or just sheer display. We are told how, at the opening of one theatre, the procession of captives, animals, and treasure, supposedly taken at Troy, was so long in passing that the actual play was never reached.

Most typical of Roman Imperial theatre, was the *pantomimus,* an actor who performed without speech, while a large chorus sang and danced the episodes that he portrayed. Such actors reached a high degree of technical skill and " mime " (in the limited modern sense and as preserved in French tradition) must owe much to them. The vast troupes of dancing girls (supported at state expense) and the general wealth of the theatre in the later Empire depended on the popularity of such " spectacular " shows.

Early Christians were specially warned against the " spectacles " for their supposed immorality and sensuous appeal.

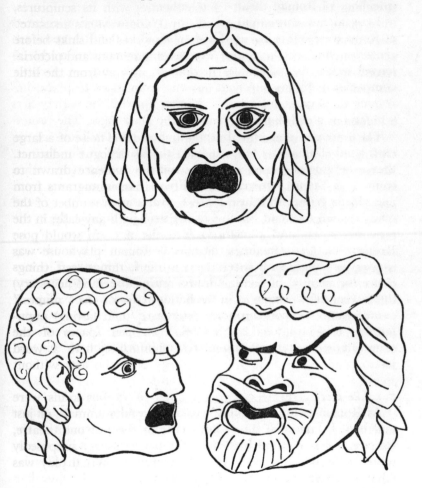

FIG. 21.—Masks in classical western theatre. Tragic hero. Youth. Servant.

Curiously the word is now again familiar to us as a method of presenting variety turns acceptable to modern taste, the " spectacular ", used again as a noun. The Roman anticipated modern efforts. When one remembers that orchestra space came back into use, sometimes for presenting sea-battles with actual ships, sometimes for wild beast shows, sometimes for the trained dancers and mimetic movement, one begins to realise (in terms of the great size of the theatre) something of the massive splendour of Roman theatre production.

Long after the apparent fall of the Western Empire, theatres at Rome were still being used and repaired in the fifth and sixth centuries. But the large and expensive presentations could no longer secure the patronage needed or state support. Smaller companies of mimes survived, touring from place to place, becoming the servants of a noble, joining up with the variety acts who also tramped the rutty roads of the Dark Ages. The professional is tough; somehow he maintained the traditions of his craft until drama was re-born from the liturgy of the church; then, emerging he joined with the companies of actors in such a country as France, where church drama moved out into yards and village greens, to infuse his own professionalism (rough and ready though that had become in the struggle to meet the crude taste of barons and peasantry) into the new theatre of the Renaissance. Or, sometimes, he may be found with wandering singers, sometimes with entertainers in the fairgrounds. The evidence for survival of secular drama (surprising enough in centuries when all writing was in the hands of clerics of one kind or another) and the contemporary references to " *mimi seu joculatores* " may be studied in Sir E. K. Chambers' *The Mediaeval Stage*. Early chapters contain interesting information on this subject.

7. *The Dark Ages*

As Roman polity gradually weakened, and yet was absorbed and used by national states formed from the provinces of the Empire, a new cultural force took the place of the scholars and writers of Rome; it was the Church, more especially the Roman Church associated with the Pope, which was now the guardian of order and education. The Christian Bishop took over, in the fifth century, much of the authority of Roman secular rule. This emerges clearly in the writing of, for example, Sidonius, once Imperial administrator, later Bishop and defender of his see city against invading barbarians. At first, these churchmen were often scholarly persons who retained the attitudes and tastes of cultured Greco-Roman thought; despite the later emphasis on the churchmen who opposed theatre, others (now forgotten) were enthusiasts for the drama. In like manner a German abbess of the eighth century composed Christian plays after the manner of Plautus to be acted, perhaps, by her nuns on festal occasions. Hroswitha was only the more articulate evidence of the persistent classical culture; a study of Sir E. K. Chambers' *Mediaeval Drama* will show the survival of the mime and the variety actor. In the east, of course, under the Byzantine emperors, dramatic tradition was unbroken, even if gradually weakened, remaining to be taken over by Turkish conquerors centuries later.

In Europe the decay of theatre was due not so much to the opposition of the church as to the gradual loss of culture; city communities no longer flourished as centres of artistic endeavour in the Dark Ages of the ninth and tenth centuries, save where (in Italy) urban life was so strongly established that it could adapt itself to new patrons and new demands; an aristocracy, born from the invaders, had little sympathy with, or love for, the finer arts. Indeed, they had regarded theatre as something associated with Roman decadence and effeminacy. So their Christianity tended to equate religious duty (which makes for strength secured from God's favour) with hatred of more refined feelings. Their attitude is parallelled in our own day by those who attempt to secure acknowledgment of their virility by studied contempt for culture, especially emotional or artistic expression; the veneer of civilisation wears thin, and " Vandal " ancestry reveals itself. Contrast the attitudes in the older civilisation of the east; significant differences are at once plain. Similarly, churchmen coped with the turbulent barons and uneducated peasantry only by meeting them on their own ground. We may parallel the decline of culture generally with that gradual narrowing of religious faith and practice indicated by comparing a typical mediaeval scholar with the Christian writers of the fifth century. In any case, civilisation had, as it were, to strip itself to the bare essentials to face the most devastating onslaught of all, the raids and devastations of the Northmen. Where culture had survived, in Ireland, or had developed again, as in England, these clumsy and unheroic murderers almost succeeded in destroying all organised community life. Nevertheless, somehow the secular entertainer survived. A fresh development of theatre was needed, from its traditional source, the ritual of religion, ritual itself derived from dramatic enactments and presentations. The old religion and theatre being in decay, the victorious Christian religion had to (I say " had to " since drama of some kind is a human necessity) develop a new drama. Yet we must not forget that Christianity did include and fulfil much earlier religious practice. So, too, the new drama depended on much that had gone before and was readily syncretist in its development, content, and conventions.

From the drama of the Mass developed the new theatre, perfectly exemplifying the two-fold methods of dramatic growth, (a) the central act which expands by adding detail and involving other related acts, (b) the story which is gradually dramatised and meets the expanding dramatic intent of the ritual. So first, to the showing forth of Christ's death, resurrection, and everliving Presence, are added the " tropes " which expand and make more explicit this presentation. Secondly, other Bible stories, not so closely involved, seem relevant; as the tropes expand into dramatic form, such stories legitimately and inevitably receive dramatic treatment. Linked with the evolving drama is, of course, music, chant, and intoned dialogue. The first theatre is the church itself, the second, the courtyard or steps leading to the main doors, the third, the churchyard, and then the town square or the village green. The student will notice that we have here the same overall pattern as in Greece, Japan, India, China, despite distinctions of detail and emphasis. Theatre and drama in all countries are basically similar in origin, intent, and modes of development, however fascinating their national peculiarities.

8.   *European Theatre—Germany*

Here, as we should expect, since it was one of the last countries (all in all) to be Christianised, never effectively part of the Empire, the pagan dramatic traditions in folk-play and local festival, were stronger, perhaps, than in many other parts of Europe. During the middle ages the Fastnachtspiel—the Carnival Play of the Feast of Fools—with its ribaldry and licence survived from pagan seasonal observances. Here we have once again the origin of comedy, social comment and adjustment in dramatic play, as in other European countries. Secular farces are also found, evidence of the less narrowly ecclesiastical activities of high-spirited young students and clerics in holiday mood. Satiric intent is strongly marked in Germanic writing—and not least in the secular drama. The theatre was simple. A stage was erected on a cleared space; the characters paraded on together; each in turn identified himself as he entered the action. Meanwhile the church drama had developed within the framework of ritual. In Germany, however, the ecclesiastical drama did not emerge so clearly or powerfully into performances beyond the church precincts, possibly because there was no very strong existing dramatic culture (other than the apparently non-religious or pagan) to help it to further development. Contrast conditions in France.

We must mention now the next development in European drama, the revival (by scholars and, in some sense, artificially) of earlier classical drama and theatre. In Germany this came, as it were, from outside its own traditions; this was so in varying degrees in other countries, but less so in France and Italy; in the former the mimetic tradition had never died; in the latter there was continuity, however tenuous, with classical ideals, as a study, say, of Petrarch's letters will show. In Germany manuscripts of Terence and Seneca were studied at Heidelburg from 1480 onwards, and inevitably were imitated both in active performance and in dramatic writing. Again, the involved political and religious strife which destroyed the older order in Germany through the first three decades of the sixteenth century gave political slant and satiric purpose to plays which stemmed from the secular farces and carnival plays mentioned above. (There was a parallel development in England, though less notable in the much greater overall dramatic activity in our own country.) However, theatre had now come to use the hall with platform imported from Italy, where a kind of " classical " stage suitable for the performance of Terence had been in use from the mid-fifteenth century.

A significant advance came from an organiser and director of carnival plays, the famous Hans Sachs of Nuremburg, master cobbler, master of ceremonies, master singer. He took over the disused Martha Kirche, and placed a simple stage across one end (plays were normally set in the open air). As with the hall stage (of school or University drama) the audience sat facing the platform, not on three sides. Here, then, various traditions begin to coalesce. Yet Germany was behind Britain, for example, in the development of theatre. The visits of touring English companies, from our own Elizabethan theatre, encouraged the German native drama. The English set up their own Elizabethan form of

K

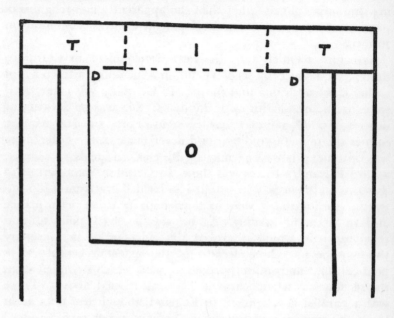

stage—an important witness to the necessity of providing dramas with the stage and conventions for which they were written—and evidenced in their presentation their powers of improvisation and mime, filling out, where appropriate, words which the local audience would have difficulty in following, if indeed they could understand them at all.

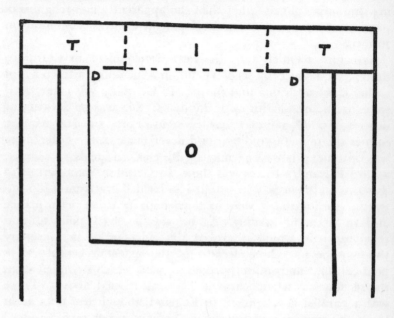

FIG. 22.—Simplified sketch plan of early Elizabethan platform stage. T—tiring house.   I—inner stage.   D—doors

By the mid-seventeenth century, after the visits of these companies, there were in Germany three main forms of theatre. (a) The Court drama, drawing still further (as early scholarly Renaissance and University plays had done) on the revived " classical " theatre of Italy and the new machinery and scenic devices that had there developed. (b) A continuing native tradition of strolling companies, now to be regarded as professional entertainers, however simple their material, and (c) the new church plays, or rather theological drama, consciously used by the Jesuits as an educational medium and instrument of the counter-Reformation. Yet this was not mere propaganda; it was also effective theatre, provided as an aid to communal thought and enterprise which was religious in basis. It was the fulfilment, in dramatic terms, of the Catholic way of life. Just as pagan plays arise in pagan life, so ecclesiastical drama accompanies a believing Christian community.

Germany, however, showed little evidence of a *strong* native impulse. French influence, regarded as civilising, was powerful in the eighteenth century. Neo-classical drama, and the narrower critical views of Voltaire, were favoured by authority. It is not until Schlegel, Lessing, and Schiller, that we find the cultivation of native German themes, the attempt to encourage emotional expression, and (in some way) to do for the Germanic spirit what Shakespeare had done for England. Shakespeare became a releasing impulse for many European countries. In him was dramatic life; they attempted to follow, however woodenly, or with whatever misunderstanding. Later, emotion is given free expression, and native German inspiration, even in exaggeration, fantasy, and pagan force (and beings—trolls, wood-spirits, spectres), emerges in the *sturm und drang* period. Romantic plays set in forest or mediaeval castle had a great impact on British theatre during the early nineteenth century. The *Götz von Berlichingen* (1773) of Goethe is regarded—in its boldness, emotional force, and disregard of the Unities—as an important stage in the movement. Here is a typical drama of revolt, the " hero " set against conventional social order. In Schiller's themes, *Don Carlos* (1787), *Wallenstein* (1799), *Maria Stuart* (1800), *Die Jungfrau von Orleans* (1802), *and Wilhelm Tell* (1804) we have romantic struggle fully exploited in typical themes.

France

France contrasts with Germany; here we have a part of the old Roman Empire that never entirely lost, especially in the South, its classical culture. Further, the place of France within the cosmopolitan world of the Empire meant that its folk traditions were weaker than those of Germany, or even of England; the folk drama had correspondingly less influence. We are dealing with a more sophisticated community; the mimes and professional entertainers were still performing in the later fifth century, and soon re-emerge after the Dark Ages to work with new drama inspired by Church Liturgy.

This " new drama ", because in an environment more congenial to theatre, soon moved from the actual Church building to outside performance. Even an Anglo-Norman mystery was thus located, reflecting French influence, in the twelfth century. Its actual presentation, near to the church, possibly on the stone platforms furnished by the church steps, has analogies with the early Shinto drama in the precincts of temples. France soon exploited the possibilities of Church drama in another direction. While the Bible stories seemed at first to afford few opportunities for introducing ordinary, everyday, events and people, the lives of Saints, once accepted as suitable extensions of liturgical drama, were not so limited. Saints could, and did, travel anywhere; in fact, the more worldly the temptations, the more honestly earthy or urban the places in which they worked, the greater their saintliness in remaining sinless. So in the *Jeu de St. Nicolas* (13th century) Jean Bodel is able (almost) to present a secular drama. The minor clergy and students joined with the survivors of the mimes (now minstrels, jesters, composers of satiric and secular love poetry, as well as the writers in the " romance " tradition, powerful in so cultured a land as France) to exploit the opportunity for amusement, social and ecclesiastical criticism, and general revelry, which the presentation of plays could easily encourage. They formed brotherhoods, temporary at first but later serious and lasting organisation, the " sociétés joyeuses ". Secular farces and folk plays also existed, more sophisticated and more theatrically developed than in Britain, such as the *Jeu de Robin et Marion,* familiar enough names, of the 13th century. Staging was more commonly round a fixed open space or platform, mansions or houses being provided at the back or sides of this. Such *décor simultané* survived into the sixteenth century in the Hotel de Bourgogne.

The Confraternity of the Passion was working in 1402, presenting mystery plays in an indoor " theatre ", and, apparently (as elsewhere) also satiric morality drama, the " soties ", or topical skits. In such an organisation the semi-professional is almost certain to emerge. Equally, the link with the Church, which objected to the mingling of broad farce and bawdy wit with sacred drama, was almost certain to be broken. At all events, the native drama is evidently established when such a play as *Maître Pierre Patelin* can be produced in 1470.

The Renaissance effort, initiated in Italy, to revive classical theatre was naturally, in its earlier stages, more pleasing to scholars than to professionals. But such early plays as Étienne Jodelle's *Cléopâtra captive* soon encouraged drama of more contemporary relevance both in theme and presentation such as Antoine de Montchrétien's *L'Ecossaise,* on the theme of Mary Queen of Scots, in 1603. On the other hand, this *commedia erudita* was parallelled by the *commedia dell'arte,* the theatre of the professional, for travelling companies, inspired by Italian comedians, were now truly professional; the ancient " comedy of masks " was again popular.

But it was hard to establish such professional theatre in the capital. The only recognised place of performance was the Hôtel de Bourgogne, belonging to the Confraternity of the Passion. Strolling players could secure acting space only within fair-grounds and at times of public holiday. The popularity of the secular drama in France, and its power as an influence in the community (for reasons advanced above) was necessarily met by firm and at times relentless control from the authorities, whether ecclesiastical—outlawing actors—or by royalty—anxious to shape theatre its own way.

By royal permission Jean-Baptiste Poquelin eventually established himself in Paris; as an actor and playwright, reared in the *commedia dell'arte* tradition, Poquelin and his fellows found favour (eventually) with the king by court performances, and were then allowed to remain at the Petit-Bourbon, which they shared with a *commedia* company associated with Scaramouche. Poquelin, sometimes using *commedia* themes, delineated the life of the day, as known in court circles. He caught the whims and manners of the moment, satirised the deviations within society which might be harmful, and thus became the first writer of the true " comedy of manners ". The king found in such a dramatic activity a valuable and healthy social function, restraint, through clear presentation of follies (in all their stupidity and ugliness), of anti-social trends. But the comedy of manners is more than this; it can exist only when there is a society sufficiently stable to have such established canons of taste and behaviour, manners accepted so that subtle deviation is noticeable and regarded. The social sin, rather than the human folly, is its satiric object. The king, after the years of anarchy, laboured to impose a civilised and urbane code of courtly behaviour. For him the work of Molière, as Poquelin is better known, was not only diverting, but positively good and socially desirable. And, indeed, here was one of the functions of comedy, the cleansing of society. It is said that Louis even suggested some of the characters to be satirised;

at his request the garrulous huntsman was added in *The Impertinents*.

However, this comedy of manners was mingled with less "legitimate" entertainment, At court the *comédie ballets* were popular. Between acts, spectacles, dances, and mask-like ballets, in which courtiers participated, were popular. More legitimate drama (itself often little removed from the *commedia* in characters, however these might be modified to accord with contemporary fashion or personality) had to be presented, an act at a time, sandwiched between such "ballets". It affords an amusing if fortuitous parallel with its forerunner in the "comedy of manners" *genre*, the plays of Menander, where, after an act, a papyrus notes "something for the chorus", denoting the insertion of unrelated dance, song, and (perhaps) spectacle. Meanwhile, the erudite and scholarly tragedy had approached the needs of the professionals. But it had still scholarly ideals; limitations were placed on it by the dramatic theorists of the time. Yet in the new "Romanity" and cultural "establishment" fostered by the king, it could find a welcome. Classical control, classical decorum, was acceptable both in society and in theatre; so the two trends, of classical scholar and social need, united.

The movement towards a more flexible interpretation of classical rules, which seemed possible with such a play as *L'Ecossaise*, was halted, curiously, by one of the greatest plays of the century, which made its author's reputation, Corneille's *Le Cid*. The theme was too "romantic" (in the later sense of the word), too unrestrained, too free in action and emotion; the great dramatist returned in later dramas to such neo-classic themes as *Horace* and *Cinna*. His later contemporary, Racine, still holds the stage with such "classical" tragedies as *Iphigénie* and *Phèdre* (1677). Melodious and beautifully constructed couplets, the dignity and poise of the actors, real emotion, controlled and expressed with classical beauty and reticence, ensure that the French classical tragedy, the result of various influences, but most of all perhaps of the essential "Romanity" of French culture, survives as part of world theatre. Perhaps only the French genius and the French language could use successfully such a controlled form of dramatic expression, based on conventions, such as the Unities, and laws which in themselves are probably irrelevant to drama.

Despite later irruptions of *sturm und drang*, and English

actors who presented the " barbarian " Shakespeare (as Voltaire termed him), with the resulting spate of romantic plays which (typically) took as their heroes outlaws from society (such as Hugo's *Hernani* in 1830) the true French dramatic tradition is best found in classical tragedies, and in the carefully preserved acting methods of the Comédie-Française; polish, wit, style, cultural continuity and aesthetic values, are gifts which France brings to European drama. The classical basis of their theatre is still evident, a framework, an accepted store of plots and dramatic " myths " to which they can always return as did the ancient Greeks, whether in Giradoux' *Amphitryon 39*, Sartre's *The Flies,* or Anouilh's *Antigone.*

One other inheritance from classical (and especially Roman) antiquity thrives healthily in France as the film *Les Enfants du Paradis* so eloquently reminded us, the art of mime (in the narrower sense), presented most typically today by Marcel Marceau and his companies.

Italy

Italy, more than any other country, as might be expected, unites, in its traditions and practice, the old with the new, the classical with the modern theatre. Church drama developed much as in other countries, but, in the " Laudi " of the mid-thirteenth century, there was a distinctive dramatic impulse derived from the " Flagellanti ". Devotional praise, at first lyric, became narrative, and then involved impersonation. Remaining choral in basis, episodes were arranged and presented in due order to illustrate the festivals of the Church year, varying from district to district. Those of Umbria and the Abruzzi are preserved in manuscripts of the sixteenth century.

Another distinct dramatic form was the " Sacre Rappresentazioni ". In 1454 at Florence the St. John's Day festival included a procession of clergy and religious guilds, who presented various events of the Old and New Testaments. Fraternities and schools acted the episodes in refectories or on open air stages with *décor simultané.* Gradually secular elements—even satiric comment on Church matters—were introduced. Stories—not religious in origin—were used in miracle plays, as in France, on the lives of Saints. Some influence from these plays persisted in the scholarly drama of the Renaissance, especially in plays of the counter-Reformation. Music, spectacle, comedy, and serious action, blended in a form not unlike eastern theatre in its comprehensive theatrical appeal.

In minstrels, acrobats, and acted dialogues, a surviving secular tradition may be traced, active at festival times among rural communities. Whether it is possible, on the existing evidence, to regard the *commedia dell'arte* as a survival from the Atellan farces of Roman times, as some have contended—pointing to similarities in characters and masks—is dubious; but the existence of vigorous rural farce from which the *commedia* emerged is not in doubt; actor dramatists such as Calmo and Beolco developed its possibilities in the early sixteenth century.

Even more important for western theatre, however, was the conscious revival by cultured writers of the forms of classical tragedy and their ideas on the laws which (quoting Aristotle) they believed should govern drama. Mussato (late thirteenth century) and Manzini, in the fourteenth century, composed Latin " tragedies " in the style of Seneca. Vernacular tragedy appeared with Caminelli's *Filostrato e Panfile* (1499) based on Boccaccio's *Tancred and Gismond*. During the sixteenth century the new knowledge of, and enthusiasm for, Greek inspired the attempt to approximate even more closely in vernacular plays to classical models. Trissino's *Sofonisba* (1524) has chorus, act division, and unity of time, and so establishes a pattern. The necessary compromise with professional theatre, ministering to a larger audience than scholarly enclaves, began with the addition to such classical plays of inter-act ballet and spectacle. Then, also in the early sixteenth century, scene perspectives and effects began (quite unclassically) to dominate presentation.

Giambattista Giraldi (1504-73) starting with Senecan grimness in such works as *Orbecche,* moving to less uniformly horrifying plays in *Dido* and *Cleopatra,* presented in *L'Altile* a dramatised mediaeval story, in which the characters were not royal and to which there was a happy ending. As some other dramatists, he seems to have realised that Aristotle's statements were not necessarily relevant to the theatre of his own day. But the neo-classical pattern was not greatly changed, although many more romantic stories were made the subjects of serious plays. With such varied plots and material, tragi-comedy developed, and even plays on contemporary themes, such as Savarro's treatment, in the early seventeenth century, of the lives of Anne Boleyn and Mary Stuart—preceding many other dramas on that unfortunate queen. At the same time "Senecan" drama continued with Speroni's *Canace* (1543). The Jesuits encouraged religious drama in the seventeenth century; one feels the influence of the *sacra rappresentazione* in such a play as Andreini's *L'Adamo* (1613). Important in its influence, Italian classical tragedy was not a continuing force in its own right. The Senecan originals ceased to be produced, and tragedy merged (as we shall note) with other forms.

Pastoral plays, using an approach popularised by Tasso, provided, in mythological themes, a style of drama which could utilise developing spectacle, and enlist already existent court "maskings" and dances. This was a congenial element in the classical inheritance. Becarri's *Il Sacrifizio* (1555), Argenti's *Lo Sfortunato* (1568), Tasso's *L'Aminta* (acted at Ferrara in 1573), led on to the much more ambitious *Il Pastor Fido* of Guarini in 1598. The Arcadian world then blends into the scenic splendour and music drama of the seventeenth century.

Italy's greatest achievement was, perhaps, in the *commedia erudita*. We have referred already to the revivals of Plautus and Terence (on a stage which formed a compromise between mediaeval house conventions and simple classical platforms backed by entrances) starting, in a sense, with student plays of the later fourteenth century such as the *Paulus* of Vergeria (c. 1389). Such dramas, rough, satiric, aimed at topical follies, began to take into themselves elements from classical plays which were then being copied and adapted. In Piccolomini's *Chrysis* the classical type characters are discernible. By 1430 many of Plautus' plays were known. But there was not yet a union between the *entertainment* and the *play*, with its continuing educational and moral emphasis; inter-act spectacles and dances were necessarily added to amuse, while courts of princes and churchmen competed in splendour. It was left to Ariosto (1474-1533) to unite the Plautine comic basis with popular story, and to secure realistic presentation of contemporary human follies. Almost suddenly, there emerges in *Cassaria* (1508) a synthesis which achieves full theatre, followed by the *I Suppositi* (1509); other writers such as Cardinal Bibbiena (*La Calandria,* 1506) worked in the same genre. Machiavelli (1469-1527) used Terence's work for *L'Andria,* that of Plautus for *La Clizia,* while his original *La Mandragola* utilises dialogue to reveal character with almost diabolical precision. Aretino (1492-1556) was a prolific writer with comic power, through whose plays, such as *La Cortegiana* (1525), *L'Ipocrito* (1542), and *Il Filosofo* (1544), bustling characters parade, intrigue, and struggle.

Herein lay the general contribution of Italian "erudite" comedy as it met and influenced the professional theatre of Europe. Gosson summarised its themes unkindly as "Love, cosenedge, flatterie, bawderie, slye conveighance of whordome . . . the persons cookes, queanes, knaves, baudes, parasites", and more in the same vein.

We have referred briefly to the possible origin of the *commedia dell'arte*. Though it found its way into the courts of princes, its life impulse was the open air world of the professional stroller. It was not, however, without help from people whose main career was not acting or entertainment. At carnival time, for example, Angelo Beolco left his task as a manager of family estates and, with the aid of friends, took to presenting plays. Himself adopting the mask of a talkative Paduan, he devised other such "masks" for his friends. His written plays, using Plautine material, survive. But the great actors of the *commedia dell'arte* depended for their effect and distinctive quality on improvisation from a given synopsis; their skill lay in adopting material to audience and occasion. Tricks and skills were passed on, partially at least, to those who inherited (within a given company or area) their work and "mask". Further, although the individual may "devise" or vary mask types, it is observable that (as those who seek to align the *commedia* with Atellan farce note) there is a continuing pattern of "types", the drolls or eccentrics who recur in society, a pattern which is more or less permanent.

Further, in more successful companies of the early seventeenth century, members played together as a team, utilising the conventions of each mask. A full company might include two "parents", Pantaleone, the avaricious and irascible Venetian business man, and the lawyer from Bologne, Dr. Graziano, who had something in common with the pedantic scholars of Elizabethan comedy, less forceful than Pantaleone, though he could talk most eloquently, often in muddled gibberish. The lovers are idealistic abstractions; they wore no masks, and their laments, soliloquies, and *pazzie*, needed careful delivery. Actresses may be said to have made their way (generally speaking) into professional theatre through the *commedia dell'arte*, in which they were an important part of the travelling group, often as wives of the actors.

The " captain "—braggart and rascally coward—would imitate the manners of unpopular foreign soldiers. Sometimes a rival to the lover, he was, in the end, an important character in his own right, associated with the great Francesco Andreini in the late sixteenth and early seventeenth century. The " zanni " or servants inherited the tasks of the slaves in classical comedy; they exemplify the syncretism of theatre. In towns, Bergomask *facchini* were amusing rogues who gained a living in any way possible, ready to do anything that offered profit. Bergomask pronunciation of the common name Gianni, familiar form of Giovanni, was " Zanni "—and this became the generic name for these lumpish, worldly, unscrupulous, and amusing, servants—whether Arlecchino, Pedrolino, Brighella, or Pulcinella—later Punch, that representative of rural Neopolitan wit and cunning. The influence of the *commedia* was wide. We have already indicated its developments in France, and there are many links with its characters in Elizabethan and later English comedy.

Finally, we must note Italy's approach to " total " theatre in the " opera ", a word of loose connotation, varying in meaning from century to century. Obviously music, song, and dance, are part of the theatrical presentation, even if not always used. But the more specific origin of what we now call " opera " has been found by some historians in the *Camerata* of Florence, a brotherhood of aristrocrats and poets who desired, among other things, the revival of Greek tragedy which (they recognised) had been largely sung or chanted. Short plays were written in what they thought was an acceptable convention, with music and singing, to imitate classical drama, such as the *Euridice* (always a favourite operatic theme) of Rinuccini and Peri (1600).

In Monteverdi's *Orfeo* the music, hitherto subordinate to the words, assumed more importance as a dramatic medium. The resulting form developed—an opera house was opened in Venice in 1637. Other cities followed with special theatres for this new music-drama, which moved quickly to involved and lavish productions from such a comparatively simple start. Before 1700 more than 350 operas had been staged in Venice alone. Scenery and spectacular effect were now, almost inevitably, the accompaniment of the grand classical themes, the stage crowded with the large cast and chorus singers. Libretti were, in fact, often devised just to allow the machinists and scene artists full scope. Again, to meet popular taste, the writers moved on from Greek and Roman themes to Oriental and Nordic subjects, inevitably concerned with the great and the demi-gods, although historic events were also used, starting perhaps with Monteverdi's *In- coronazione di Poppea* in 1642.

Opera spread to Vienna, where under Ludovico Burnacini (1636-1707) were seen some of the most beautiful examples of baroque stage settings. German Courts followed the example of Vienna, and set up their own opera houses and resident com- panies. By the early eighteenth century Italian opera was known and performed in every European country. Under Alessandro Scarlatti, Naples became a centre of future operatic training and development. From here many singers were sent out into various European countries. Virtuosity of vocal production dominated other considerations now. Something was then inevitably lost from the " total theatre " achieved when all elements in produc- tion blend for entire dramatic effect. At its greatest, grand opera is perhaps the nearest successor we have to the comprehensive appeal of classical Greek tragedy, uniting all human faculties, perceptions, and desires, in a complete " experience " of the life we live, the environment we share, the universe in which we move and strive. Gluck's preface to his *Alceste* (1767) enforces a personal attempt to return again to fuller music drama, in con- trast to exercises in vocal skills.

Comic opera developed in Naples by the addition of scenes calculated to amuse the local audience. Such scenes, at first added to the Venetian operas, became after a time intermezzi, independent of the main plot, plays in themselves. So we have Pergolesi's *La Serva Padrona* (1733). By 1752, an *opéra comique* was established in Paris, linking with earlier ballad opera presentation or *pièces en vaudeville*. In another direction, the new comic opera utilised other forms of professional theatre, especially the *commedia dell'arte*, through the work of Goldoni; stock characters are introduced even in Mozart's *Magic Flute*, although given distinctive vitality by their musical rôles.

Increasing fantasy and mysticism in European opera looked forward to the romanticism of the nineteenth century. Subse- quent development of musical plays in their multifarious variety —comic opera of various conventions (on to Gilbert and Sulli- van), surviving ballad operas, melodramas (when music was utilised sometimes in early nineteenth century Britain to avoid infringing the monopoly of the " patent " theatres) comedies with music, musical comedies (again of differing styles), opera bouffé, vaudevilles, burlesque—may be studied with operatic conventions in mind as well as consideration of the non-musical plays to which music was added. (Notice the many operatic versions of Shakespeare and the romantic novels of Scott.) All forms are flexible, changeable, constantly varying and adapting their emphasis within the overall tasks and aims of theatre.

The *commedia dell'arte* toured Europe. Their influence passed into various national theatres and is with us today. With the establishment of settled resident companies (we have noted, for example, how Molière's strollers with their *commedia* background became influential in professional theatre, merging with the " erudite " tradition), the touring companies lost both personnel and incentive. Goldoni, in the eighteenth century, converted the *commedia* into a more polished form, composing complete plays, witty and relevant to contemporary life; however fantastic his plots, Gozzi used the *commedia* convention for satire, still allowing scope for improvisation. The decay of the *commedia dell'arte* poses some interesting problems—the precise rôle of actor and dramatist, and their method of collaboration. Improvisation may break down into a series of tricks based on earlier *lazzi;* on the other hand, an untheatrical writer will shackle and destroy the actor's power and art. The writer really needs, himself, to be a man of theatre, knowing that his script is part— and only part—of the actor's equipment; he must write with his theatre, its conventions and audience, in mind.

The student may be able to perceive these various influences in later development of Italian (and European) theatre. We must remember the persistence of the regional spirit (evidenced above) in Italian drama, seen even after the achievement of political unity—the Venetian comedy of Gallina (*Serenissima,* 1891), the Sicilian *Cavelleria Rusticana* of Verga (1840-1922), the Milanese dialect plays of Bertolazzi (1870-1916) and Novelli's *Il Cupolone* (1913), Florence in the *quattrocento.* The reality of, and affection for, Italian provincial life has also been evidenced in recent films.

The originality emerging from such a varied and vital intellectual background, combined with the sense of style and form implicit in a theatre steeped in classical disciplines, ensures the continuing vitality of Italian drama. The student should examine the development of the " teatro del grottesco " and the work of Pier Maria Rosso di San Secondo—such a play as his *La Scala* the opening act set on the staircase of a block of flats. Of course, he will also read (and try to see performances of) the plays of Pirandello. Especially disturbing is his *Six Characters in Search of an Author*. Here we are made to consider the " mask "—that emblem of the early actor—not only on the stage but as worn in daily life. What is the mask—and what the face? Which is real? Life becomes patterned; humans don the appropriate mask day by day. It may be, when their subconscious or their secret life is dramatically revealed in theatre, that the mask they then *actually* don may indeed be the *truth;* the daily face is the pretence and the falsity. In theatricality emerges *reality*.

Spain

A further country, the theatrical history of which has significance for western theatre as a whole, is Spain. Ecclesiastical drama developed early. A fragmentary vernacular play, the *Auto de los Reyes Magos,* dates from the mid-twelfth century. Such plays were performed at festivals. Equally, the secular farce, associated with the Roman mime tradition, had not entirely disappeared, for clergy were forbidden to participate in " juegos de escarnio "—burlesques and comic *jeux d'esprit*. The establishment of Corpus Christi as a festival in 1264 gave, as elsewhere, impetus to dramatic performances, but whereas in Britain plays were arranged in cycles, in Spain such historical sequence was (perhaps typically) subordinated to devotional purpose, beautiful staging (with built up platforms on several levels), and the expensive properties of a thematic presentation.

At the Renaissance, such earlier religious plays inspired individual writers to make complete and lengthy treatment of devotional subjects; but at court masks and shows of a more secular nature were staged (as elsewhere) with spectacular settings and costumes; the continuing " juegos " helped to stimulate the revival of classical theatre. The pastoral convention, here stemming from the shepherds in religious or morality drama, offered, as in Italy, a harmless and pious escape from mediaeval limitations of subject. So Juan del Encina (1468-c.1537), actor, playwright, musician, and servant to the Duke of Alba, composed his *Eglogas Representados en Recüesta de Amores*—the transforming power of love can change even rough shepherds. The powerful religious and devotional influence, however, continued in more fully developed plays such as Fernandez' Easter drama *Auto de la Pasion* performed in Salamanca Cathedral by clergy on Good Friday.

Bartolemé de Torres Naharro (c.1480-1530) established in critical writing and exemplified in dramatic work the distinction between comedies of manners and romantic comedies concerned with love and honour, and anticipated the work of Lope de Vega. Some plays adopt the conventional Italian street setting, seen in the designs of Serlio. Parallel, similarly, to Italian operatic experiments, dramas developed the use of music. Short pieces, *entremés*, accompanied a full length presentation; then short inter-act comic sketches (as in Encina's plays) became a distinct theatrical form in themselves, songs and musical " illustrations " combining with the action.

Through the early sixteenth century religious drama continued. Inspired, however, by free translation from Plautus, Terence, and even Euripides, attempts were made to write original plays on the classical model. Then, too, professional theatre was established, at first by touring companies of more skilled performers, and before the end of the century in permanent theatres, in Madrid, Seville, and Valencia. Life among the strolling players, their plain stage of boards, the few simple properties, can be studied from the eye-witness accounts of Cervantes and Agustin de Rojas, himself a travelling actor, in his *El Viaje Entretenido*. The reputation of the professionals was founded on vivid short prose sketches (or interludes), the comic *pasos*. As in England at much the same time, the first " theatres " were yards in which spectators stood in the open air, while others watched from the balconies of houses. Early theatre buildings retained the platform jutting into the audience. Such was the Corral de la Cruz built in 1579. A curtain at the back of the platform (compare, again, the Elizabethan playhouse) was drawn on occasion to reveal properties or objects indicative of locality. In general the scene changed at the behest of the actors' (and audiences') imagination. Again as in England, however, scenery was introduced during the next century, copying Court methods, a front curtain was added, and the resultant proscenium arch.

Cueva and Cervantes, drawing on contemporary events and

personal experience, developed dramatic skills further. The great dramatist of Spanish theatre, contemporary with Shakespeare, but outliving and holding an even more commanding position in relation to his fellows, was Lope de Vega (1562-1635). Using popular stories, the Bible, history, mythology, he developed a form of " total " theatre suited to the tradition and genius of Spanish drama, diversifying his plays with music and dancing. He was well aware that drama is action—not abstract argument. He relied little on stage machinery or effect. As in Shakespeare, events move rapidly from place to place; his lively imagination and vivid dialogue involve the audience easily in the action.

Calderon (1600-1661), while as concerned as Lope de Vega with rapid movement and plots that centre on " honour ", is a dramatist of the " baroque ". Rhetorical language, scenes contrasting by clever stagecraft, careful effects, and the calculated *coup d'oeil*, characterise his plays. He used the work of Cosmo Lotti, a famous stage machinist. Calderon also continued the tradition of religious theatre; his *autos sacramentales*, dramatic presentations of Catholic dogma, utilise the mechanics of the stage to embody and point the argument.

In the eighteenth century, French neo-classical ideals, felt even in England, were largely accepted—for a time at least—in Spain. Lope de Vega's deliberate rejection of the Unities condemned him just as much as Shakespeare's practical disregard of them. Luzan's exposition of the " classical " principles—the *Poetics*—parallels Augustan criticism in England. Theatres were rebuilt in imitation of French and Italian models. Religious *autos* were proscribed. But, again as in England, neo-classicism had little lasting success.

Emotion and imagination returned, as in the work of Francisco Martinez de la Rosa (1787-1862). While he attempted in early work to conform to the canons of neo-classicism, or even of sentimental comedy, his *Conjuracion de Venecia* (1834), is typically romantic in theme and treatment. As in Victorian England, antiquarian and picturesque remoteness (distance both in place and time) appealed in such works as Zorrilla's (1817-93) *El Zapotera y el Re* or his *Don Juan Tenorio*.

In the late nineteenth century simpler, more realistic, treatment of everyday life found greater favour than the grand romantic approach. Modern Spanish drama, however, seems to draw on all the mingled traditions and influences of its history.

Jacinto Benavente touches realism with romantic insight, truth
with humanity. The continuing devotional setting and warm
sympathy are found in Martinez Sierra; an undogmatic but fun-
damentally religious urgency, at one with the impulses of drama
in early ages, marks the work of the Quintero Brothers. Starker
social problems and sufferings are treated by Manuel Linares
Rivas and private emotional agonies by Federico Garcia Lorca.
Their drama is, further, essentially Spanish, using the thematic
patterns and folk ideology of its own country.

Scandinavia

Scandinavia, though ultimately producing in Ibsen one of the
greatest and most influential of nineteenth century dramatists,
can hardly be regarded, any more than Russia (although again
in various ways important to contemporary theatre) as a formative influence in the development or establishment of western
drama as a whole. Denmark alone shows the normal European
pattern, from folk and religious drama to " School " drama in
the sixteenth century. Here, however, as in Sweden, there was
translation and adaptation of French and German plays. Ludwig
Holberg, a Norwegian by birth, is claimed as the first dramatist
to use the Danish language, working at a time when Danish and
Norwegian cultures were in a sense united, at least politically.
His isolation and influence were such that the early eighteenth
century is sometimes styled " the age of Holberg ". Not till the
nineteenth century, however, with Bjornson and Ibsen, are there
dramatists of international repute; but these two were indeed of
outstanding importance. Ibsen's use of socially relevant themes
united with a fine sense of theatre and practical experience. As
he himself declared he was not a propagandist; he was a dramatist. He joined, however, even with acrimony, in the con-
troversies his works aroused; but he was essentially an artist of
the theatre, utilising vital human problems, relationships, and
contemporary life. As McCarthy points out, we move from
violent action on the stage to " what is happening in people's
minds ". The intense tragic struggle within four walls, or a little
town, may be vitally relevant to humanity's endless search for
harmony in living, or its struggle with conditions of existence.
Heaven and hell can lie within a suburban sitting room, as well
as in the strife of Olympus, Oresteian dilemmas, or Hercules
defying the powers of Hades. Many modern dramatists have

L

attempted to follow his lead. He saw the universal in the particular. He said, " I think it desirable to solve the problems of women's rights along with others; but that has not been the whole purpose; my task has been the description of humanity ". In this he is distinguished from " propagandist " playwrights. Drama presents life. It is left to the audience to share that experience of life and to draw what conclusions it will, *if* it will. Shaw's practice in this respect was, luckily for the survival of his plays (or some of them), greater than his declared theory, for example, that theatre was " the week day church "—although one could interpret such a statement in a wider sense to indicate the life impulse of drama.

Swedish drama did little other than reflect the work of other European countries until the explosive emergence of Strindberg (1849-1912), whose work shows a ferocious realism, utilising symbolism later (as did Ibsen's) as his response to the vastness of human experience intensified. As Ibsen also, he was a rejuvenating influence on European drama in general.

Russia

As in Sweden, so in Russia. Its earlier derivative quality is clearly presented in Nemirovitch Danchenko's account of theatre at the turn of the century, the movements that led to the foundation of the Moscow Arts Theatre, and the emergence of Stanislavski as a director, with the success of Chehov's work, already rejected by the professional theatre of the time. Few students need to be reminded of the work of these two great men, or the effect of Stanislavski's methods of actor training on the whole of western theatre, and the near reverence accorded at one time to Chehov's plays. A theatre like the Russian, comparatively unencumbered by past achievement, was able to give new impulse to dramatic work, an impulse stimulated, in the beginning, from further west, by the work of such companies as the Meiningen Players—emphasis on the importance of each member of the crowd, a completely sincere establishment of character and motive, with over-all artistic integrity and harmony of effect for each production. Chehov reflects the attitudes, falsities, and twilight wistfulness of a passing social order; yet there are, as in Ibsen, eternal human situations and attitudes. " The Cherry Orchard " may be cut down in the interests of " progress "; it may symbolise the destruction of fertility; it may be an emblem of past aristocratic domination; but it also evokes our sense of beauty—beauty which will be valued by men (whatever their political creed or country) so long as humanity persists. Again, Chehov leaves us free to enjoy in our own way his presentation of life. He saw his world with a wry and possibly sympathetic smile; his plays were intended to be comedies; he grumbled that Stanislavski " put the tears " in his plays. Studying (and repeating so far as possible) Stanislavski's directions, we realise that a play is not only a script; it is a presentation in theatre. Only thus is a play established. Certain approaches and traditions have become accepted in regard to Chehov. Such are possibly even more authoritative in our country than in Russia itself. A Russian told me (for what it is worth) that presentations of Chehov's plays in England were usually nearer in style and attitude to Russian performances of the twenties than are modern revivals there. Stanislavski's greatest contribution to theatre lay, perhaps, in his analysis and preparation of the actor's work as he undertakes a character role. Over-emphasis on this achievement and pre-occupation with various " Method " schools, which often distort Stanislavski's approaches, over-stressing one aspect, needs to be corrected by study of his work as a whole. Read, for example, *Stanislavsky produces Othello*. Then, set this against the wider background of theatre, first in modern Soviet Russia, and then in the world beyond.

9. *Presentation and Conventions*

Necessarily, we have glanced at staging as we noted the overall dramatic development of various parts of Europe, for a play script can become drama only in the context of its actual performance, settings, and audience.

From the normal patterns of liturgical space, platform stage, various acting levels (familiar in Europe as in other parts of the world) in mediaeval times, we come, at the Renaissance, to an attempt to use the platform in conformity with what were thought to be classical methods of presentation. Simple curtained entrances at the rear of the platform, used for performances of Plautus, were soon superseded by more ambitious efforts to reconstruct the classical theatre.

Across this came a fresh distraction. The " discovery " or popularising of perspective effect fascinated the Italian mind; to indulge this new taste it was necessary to develop the scenic possibilities of theatre. Familiar with "real" and often quite elaborate properties in mediaeval drama, the audience (especially wealthy patrons) felt the need of a setting equally complete. One might claim that such pictorial perspective was a distinguishing feature of European theatre after the Renaissance, an influence from which we are only gradually disengaging ourselves.

Thus when there was an attempt to re-create the classical theatre there was also a simultaneous effort to combine perspective with it. Serlio backed his platform with street scenes in perspective; his suggestions, not literally followed, had wide and lasting influence as a general principle. His perspectives were to be made of "houses", an arrangement of mediaeval mansions adjusted to the classical platform in three styles to suit comedy, tragedy, and (with tree wings) satyric drama. Palladio in the

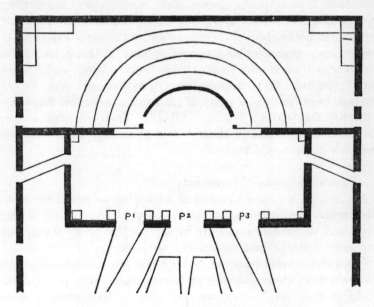

FIG. 23.—Teatro Olimpico—the beginning of the picture. Note in this sketch plan, the openings, p1, p2, p3, behind which perspectives were arranged.

Teatro Olimpico at Vicenza came nearer to Roman style architecture, with a massive stone *frons scaenae* behind the platform, and the three classical entrances. But (illustrating the dual influences of the time) behind each entrance were set, again,

" houses " in perspective. So important did the scenes behind the entrances become that the centre arch was enlarged to a wider view. Then it was allowed to extend across the whole proscenium —the two side entrances were swallowed. We had now, albeit at the back of the platform, a proscenium arch. Further, the actors, instead of performing in front of the entrances and on the platform, might move within the scenes and still be easily visible. The platform might well cease to be the real " stage ". The Teatro Farnese illustrates this further development.

At kings' courts, the ostentation which encouraged scenic display, linked with dances and royal occasions, festivals, and maskings, gave further encouragement to lavish setting. The Jacobean

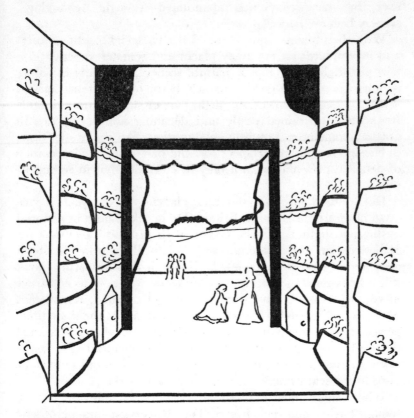

FIG. 24.—Impression of an early nineteenth century theatre in England. Based on a drawing of Drury Lane. The picture is now almost established and framed.

Court masques in England could use both platform and hall together as acting space, and the maskers moved out into the
general assembly. But a second typical western development was
technological skill, sheer delight in machinery, which had in
theatre a delightful venue for display. In any case, scenery now
demanded conflagrations, earthquakes, and transformations, to
impress foreign visitors or gain royal approbation and patronage. Mythological themes needed heaven set in " cloudings ";
Olympus in the western world was scaled by stage carpenters
and magic contrived by material means. During the seventeenth
century generally this court emphasis on setting moved (in modified professional adaptations) into public theatres. Often, however, full perspective was abandoned—though " changing "
scenery became normal.

With the romantic movement of the later eighteenth century,
and its emphasis on far away places and remoter experience, a
new pictorialism developed; natural scenery, especially in wilder
regions where the typical romantic hero, outlaw, rebel against
urban and social convention, might live, or supernatural visitants
frequented the ruined castle and declining abbey, led to still
greater, sometimes fantastic, elaboration. At the same time,
public interest in, and respect for, the past demanded accuracy
of detail in presentation, not only in costumes, but in setting itself.

De Loutherbourg, Capon, and Planché, in the years 1770-
1840 illustrate the trend in Britain. De Loutherbourg in pictorial
setting and lighting effects, Capon with historical accuracy for
Shakespearian presentations, and finally Planché with literal
accuracy in costume and detail. Although flats and wings were
still a basis for stage setting, the tendency was now to construct
more " set-pieces ", three dimensional and " solid ", reminiscent
of the expensive effects of earlier court dramas. At the same time,
perspective in scene painting was firmly established in professional
theatre by the mid-nineteenth century. The pictorial view back-
cloth, so carefully executed at that time, is still familiar to most
of us in musical comedy or operatic scenery today,

While more literal pictorial décor was encouraged by
romantic plays and melodrama, Tom Robertson (among others)
was, in the 1860's, demanding naturalistic accuracy in *interior*
settings. The wings and shutters were to be abandoned for a
" real " room with " real " doors. So came the " box " setting,

introduced possibly by Vestris, but established as a principle by Robertson and the Bancrofts who produced his dramas. Squire Bancroft gave himself the credit for achieving the first complete " picture frame " by his reconstruction of the Haymarket in 1880. With this was associated the theory of the " fourth wall ", according to which we, the theatre audience, remove (in imagination) the fourth wall fitted into the proscenium frame and " look in on " events of " actual " life in the room beyond, the other three walls established by the box set.

Fig. 25.—Formal " ritual " tragic costume in early eighteenth century England. Quin as Coriolanus.

By many, the two types of setting suggested above would still be accepted as normal western practice. But since 1900 (and earlier in many instances) there has been a return to fuller and more flexible practice and to the more traditional arts of theatre. The cinema has shown that " pictorialism " alone does not constitute theatre. For one thing, the cinema can *reach* naturalistic presentation and the illusion of normal life *(in this way)* much more completely than " live " theatre. Yet live theatre clearly possesses much that film can never achieve. Men were forced to consider what these other qualities, the essentials of theatre were. Obviously they did not depend on naturalistic accuracy or (necessarily) on elaborate setting. Further, cinema itself used *montage,* with special techniques of its own, to stylise, emphasise, symbolise; again " naturalism " was not enough.

Drama returned from " pictures framed " to three dimensional presentation. Craig, among others, demonstrated real theatrical setting, mass, line, space for movement, varying levels for the actors' use, dynamic use of the acting area. Appia developed lighting to stress shape, shadow, the solidity of properties and people, features, moods, dramatic grouping, and atmosphere. The open stage is again in use, and varying adaptations of the " apron ", and " theatre in the round ", or arena presentation, returned in the forties, if not earlier. For modern practice, we must refer the student to such an excellent manual as Lee Simonson's *The Art of Scenic Design.*

10.   *The Plays: The Western Contribution to Drama*

Since the aim of this handbook is to supplement existing books on our own British drama to which the student has ready access there is no intention of dealing fully with specific British (or American) theatre. We have tried to show contacts, inherent patterns shared by many lands, which place certain aspects of western dramatic work in perspective. We have tried further, to enable the student to see that dance, mime, " musicals ", variety entertainment, and straight plays, are part of one greater entity, a unity that we call theatre, however fragmented it may be in our own experience today. Throughout the handbook we have indicated, wherever possible, those elements in our practice which are related to, and develop from, universal patterns and impulses that are the creative energy of theatre.

It remains to note some distinctive and positive contributions of western theatre, and to try to exemplify these from plays. Two dramatic forms are specially important—the comedy, concerned with social adjustment, using as its material amusing, and (later) humorous, deviations from accepted or desirable behaviour patterns, satirical or kindly in treatment; while an Aristophanes may gibe at the new, a Shaw may laugh at the accepted convention; it may encourage or discourage innovation. With a faith in the " fertility " of the human community, its business is the health of society. Tragedy goes beyond such social considerations to deal with the further and greater quest of man for life itself, his relationship to, and significance in, his total environment.

As we study these two approaches to the treatment of life in the plays of western theatre, we are conscious that we have inherited another distinctive impulse—insistence, much more strongly emphasised than elsewhere in world theatre, on the importance of the individual, the motivating force of character; " character is destiny ", and shapes the dramatic struggle. Indeed, the obsession with " character ", often with an involved and detailed study of motives and background, has in our own time obscured elements in theatre which are more fundamental; it has sometimes prevented our understanding of the great dramatic works of the past and blocked our full appreciation of them as theatre. A great dramatist has presented in action truths of experience valid for all time, seeking to move from temporal to eternal; we may persistently stress irrelevant individual details (" How many children had Lady Macbeth?"), missing truth in a pseudo-naturalism which brings everything down to everyday confusion instead of enabling us to perceive, through the human event, the real drama, the greater conflict.

Yet character interest and emphasis is an integral part of theatre. Its gradual development and place in western theatre will be indicated below, inadequately, but perhaps sufficiently to start the student on a way of exploration and deeper thought. The plays chosen may illustrate some other features of western theatre. Arbitrary and unrepresentative (in the wider sense) as any such choice must be, something of the influences at work, and the nature of our higher dramatic achievements, should emerge from consideration of the dramatic works here summarised.

Aristophanes' *The Frogs* is an example of that Greek comedy which has been called " the most powerful weapon of social criticism known to the world."

Dionysos has lost his best playwrights—Sophocles and Euripides have recently died. He therefore sets out for the underworld (accompanied by his red-headed slave Xanthias) to bring back a tragic writer to earth. Since Herakles (or Hercules) had visited hell, Dionysos dresses himself up in the lion skin of that hero, and knocks on the centre door of the stage house to ask him the way. Hercules, seeing the strange figure before him, the luxurious Dionysos adorned as the strong man, breaks down in helpless laughter. (" He's afraid," comments Dionysos to the slave, who has already added some plaintive low comedy as a hardworked carrier of baggage.) Dionysos is told by Hercules the easy ways of finding the underworld—including the hemlock road, and the possibly less painful expedient of climbing to the summit of a high column, and stepping off. When they set out, Xanthias, still grumbling about the baggage, is encouraged by the sight of a funeral—perhaps the defunct (who is surely going on the same journey) will take the load. However, Dionysos fails to make a bargain. The corpse sits up abruptly and enquires " How much?" but on the final offer remarks, " Strike me living if I will," and orders his bearers to go on. The crossing of the River Styx, guarding the underworld, is effected by the boat-man Charon, who enters as if plying for hire, calling out the various " fare stages " of hell. He refuses to take Xanthias, who has to plod around the orchestra on a foot journey, while even Dionysos (" Fatty " to Charon) has to help row the boat. He and Charon pass through the Lenean marsh while the chorus of frogs chant their refrain, emulated by the annoyed Dionysos. When Xanthias joins his master a further chorus of devoted wor-shippers has also hymned and danced its way round the orchestra. Of such apparently incongruous contrasts is early drama composed. (Compare the horseplay in English religious plays; all life is sacred, and so the god is not insulted by frank-ness.) They are now before the door of the " skene " again. This time it represents the gateway of hell, kept by the fierce Aeacus. When he sees the apparent Hercules, he breaks into threats and vituperation. Dionysos cowers in fear. He orders Xanthias to take his place and to dress as Hercules. Unwillingly the slave obeys. Again the door opens, and this time a charming young lady, with pleasant memories of his previous visit, welcomes the supposed Hercules. She lures him with enticing dainties. Xanthias finally succumbs when she mentions " dancing girls ". Dionysos, perceiv-ing how things have changed, now goes back on his order; he *will* be Hercules. The episode reaches its climax with Aeacus having both whipped to find out who really is the god. For the god will not feel the pain. Each cries in agony but quickly im-provises a quotation or sentence to continue his moan of pain. Their entry into the underworld concludes the first half, the statement of the theme, the preparation for the " agon " to follow. But, first, there comes the most relevant contribution of the chorus, a news bulletin and comment on the events of the past year, one might say. This is a direct and violent attack on the Athenian leaders and the continuation of the war with Sparta. " Once leaders were good, valiant, and honest, Athenians —genuine metal. Now like the coinage, they are debased. We are ruled by mongrels without a name, foreigners of dubious extraction." So runs the general theme. It is as though on a state occasion the British Prime Minister and his colleagues should be attacked personally in ribald insult—to their faces—before the public assembly of the whole people. After a gibing climax (" Hang us at least on decent trees—if we must perish "), the second half begins; there is to be a contest between Aeschylus and Euripides to see who shall return to earth. In this the characteristics of the two writers, their ideas, and their style of writing, are exquisitely and precisely satirised, the wordy pomposity of the older man contrasting with the unmistakably typical phrasing of the younger, which enables his detractor to parody his apparent monotony. Here is the equivalent of sophisticated revue, enjoyed only if the audience are all equally aware of refinements of literary and dramatic allusion. Since everyone heard the tragedies year by year, most would " take " the points made. Aeschylus boasts that he can always insert such a pedestrian phrase as " found his oil-pot gone " into Euripides' prologues, retain the rhythm, and achieve sense—of a kind. No music hall comedian ever exploited the catch phrase better. But there is an interesting light on the way the two dramatists were regarded in their own day. They are asked to sacrifice to the gods before the " agon " starts. Aeschylus does so with traditional piety. Euripides (with scornful superiority refuses, but in the end invokes his own " gods "—the aether and his vocal cords.

Aeschylus returns to earth, for the theme is the need to recover the stalwart virtues of the past, to repudiate new cynicism and foreign leaders. Aeschylus may be wordy but he is sincere. The chorus end the play with a final personal gibe at the demagogue Cleon. They wish the audience peace. As for Cleon, let him go off and fight by himself in his far away homeland, wherever that may be.

This brief summary (for which I apologise to lovers of Greek comedy) may (in its inadequacy) lead readers to the play, perhaps in Murray's translation, with his excellent commentary.

There is much to be enjoyed, not least constant personal allusions and jests (understandable sometimes only to contemporary audience), every line pointed in some way or another. Western theatre has achieved little beyond this in comic drama, save in the development of romantic and character comedy. Here in one composition are the fantasy, the satiric play, the knockabout farce, the sophisticated revue, song and dance, and much more. Here also, clearly enough, is the comedy which is based on the " renewal ", the annual period of " plerosis " and social " kenosis ". But in larger communities such plays were too vivid, too dangerous. Over-organised and involved urban culture began to separate man from his real life and means of expression. Aristophanes suffered. His middle comedies abandon personal and intimate local attack for more general problems. In the *Lysistrata* (even before *The Frogs*) we are studying " characters " who may be representative but not identifiable so readily as people known to the audience.

So Greek comedy fairly soon came to concentrate on plot interest with typical citizens, vices and follies in general, as its material, not immediate and pressing problems within the community. This emphasis places greater responsibility on the actors as such. The chorus are no longer linked with the play plot, save as a formality. In some scripts recovered from Egypt a brief note is made at the end of an " episode " that here " something for the chorus " should be inserted. What that was mattered little. The variety " intermission " is simply a relief, an entertainment. (It is interesting to note that Molière staged comedies—with type characters similar to those in Greek drama—which had ballets inserted between acts.) Menander's *The Arbitration* is a delightful comedy of developed Greek theatre. While the actors wore " type " masks there is yet individuality in the portrayal of follies and pruderies. Curiously as it seems to some, the link with the traditional religious festival, the time of worship, festivity and licence, remains. Charisius is righteously aghast when his young bride Pamphila gives birth to a child five months after their marriage. The child is " exposed " but rescued by countrymen. Luckily—for we learn that four months before marriage, at a night festival, Pamphila, unwisely straying from her friends, had been ravished by an unknown youth. The " arbitration " reveals that the youth was Charisius, who is so to speak his own " villain ", the cause of his wife's disgrace, his own opponent.

There is, too, the interesting Habrotonon, harpist and pleasure girl, who is chosen by Charisius to alleviate his anger and wretchedness. She is by no means happy in her profession. Revelation of the long-lost father or child has become almost a joke, so often was it used (insincerely) in Victorian melodrama. Here, a revelation of Habrotonon's real birth is so contrived by preceding attitudes and probabilities, so subtly staged, that we are won over to an unlikely event. In any case, this was (when first played) almost a new theme in theatre! The chorus appear only briefly as a group of revellers at Charisius' house. We see the emergence of certain " types "—angry fathers, talkative servants, who yet have varied characteristics, even though masks may be identical to enable the audience to recognise immediately the general social place and age of the man or woman portrayed. Here, in a sense, we have the origin of the comedy of manners, for we are dealing with a society within which there is established pattern and hierarchy. We are entertained by divergences from the healthy and accepted norm. Comedy does not cease to be social comment, but its operation is more limited in range, more subtle. *Deviation* becomes the material of comedy, if we accept the behaviour conventions of this urban and (later) cosmopolitan society. Coarsened, this comedy of types becomes farce. Much of Plautus later tends to this. Sentimentalised, as in Terence, it may become the vehicle of special pleading on behalf of some special " set " in society, as the educational propaganda of Terence in the *Adelphi*. Renascent in the comedy of masks after the early fifteenth century, the *commedia dell'arte*, it again inspired much later drama, from the " humours " and urban life portrayed by Jonson to the true comedy of manners of Congreve, and later eighteenth century work. Perhaps one may see in the work of Wilde and Noel Coward recent equivalents (especially in *The Importance of Being Earnest* and *Private Lives*); the student may find the thought worth pursuit—even if he does not agree!

Let us examine, finally, the connection of Menander's play with religious origins. The festival secures the events of the plot; the child is born under the influence of the god. At the close the hope and wonder of life, the reconciling child who unites various people, is further stressed. With new life there is an inrush of Divine power. Here is the eternal Christmas hope—the better future in the next generation, the creative power, the " God " who upholds and sustains, ever renewed promise. Who can despair, or lose trust in the Life who so manifests and demonstrates Its continuing powers?

With the thought of Christmas, we may go on to consider Christian drama, with that development of character, emphasis on the individual life, that typifies western drama. One can trace the development of liturgical additions into " plays ", as performance moves from the church into the open air. Obvious openings are provided for extension of the plot; improvisation becomes written into accepted scripts. This addition and development does not occur so readily with characters unfamiliar to the actors or their way of life. The Three Kings remain remote and dignified figures, but Noah's wife becomes a scold, while the shepherds, well-known in mediaeval England with its vast sheep runs, become more and more contemporary workers, inhabitants of the immediate neighbourhood. The student is recommended to study this dramatic growth. Children, given the story of the shepherds, improvise much the same basic additions to the essential story, Further, important elements of comedy emerge, just as farce emerges in the Noah episode, tragedy in the Abraham and Isaac play of the Brome cycle, and final tragedy in the Easter story, with purgation and emergence on a new level of life for those who join in Resurrection victory.

More significant in later versions of the shepherds' play is the establishment of individuality. Earlier, the shepherds grumble about the weather, their work, their food, join in mock battle with the younger Trull, but in the play commonly known as the " Second Play of the Shepherds ", from the Wakefield Cycle, we have consistent attitudes and developed characterisation for the various actors, and an amusing plot. Roughly, only a sixteenth of the play is residual Bible story. The rest is an " original " work, although its antecedents can be found in earlier shepherd plays. The suggestion of a sheep raider is noticed in other cycles; the proximity to Scotland and border forays may have stimulated the idea further.

The first shepherd enters, and with Aristophanic bluntness (likewise under the protection of religious festival) attacks rulers who encourage the turning of fertile land into sheep farms. He voices the feelings of common man faced by the dogmatic assurances of economic theorists.

These men that are lordly : they cause the plough tarry.
That men say is for the best : we find it contrary.

Against the overlords who " make purveyance " he is equally
bitter—

> We are so lamed
> O'ertaxed and oppressed
> We are made hand-tamed with these gentlery men.

But it is also the fault of a system which allows bogus officials to
swagger through the land—

> For if a man get a paint sleeve or a broach nowadays
> Woe is him that him grieve or aught against him say !
> Dares no man him reprove, do what mastery he may.
> Yet no man believes one word that he say.

The words still have relevant bitterness and point. Then, with
true Yorkshire understatement, he asks us not to take any notice.
Drily he explains that while he is alone it helps him to " moan "
in this fashion.

The second shepherd, who has some pretensions to knowledge
and even Latin, joins him. Like an earlier philosopher he is un-
happily married, and addresses the audience of young men and
their girls in holiday mood with the directness and pithy comment of Victorian music hall, adding some local allusions (surely)
in his remark that while he and others are overladen with one
wife, it appears (strange to report) that recently some men have
taken to having two, or even more.

> Some are woe that has any.

" Be careful," he warns, " it's no good saying, ' If only I'd
known '—that won't help you. And, remember, it takes a little
while to get married—but it lasts a terrible long time."

> Thou may catch in an hour
> What shall savour full sore
> As long as thou liv'st.

Then, in vivid words that inevitably suggest a still remembered variety comedian, he describes his own wife. The third shepherd enlarges on the other topic of English conversation (we have had politics and the wife)—English weather.

> Was never since Noah's flood such floods seen,
> Wind and rain so rude, and storms so keen.

He recognises his two comrades and remarks, " We who walk the moors see some curious things around at night ", and then greets them with rough good humour. He is a younger man, and grumbles that he has to put up with hard treatment—

> We are wet and weary while master men wink.

They agree to pass the time with a song, which rounds off this part of the play.

Then Mak the sheep-stealer enters. We note the reaction of the three to him—the passive good temper of the first, the authority of the second, only gradually roused to irritation by Mak's bragging, and the constant aggression and youthful hot temper of the third—" Look after your belongings," he remarks as soon as Mak enters, and finally, in a turn of phrase still familiar, " Mak, know ye not me? By God, I could hurt thee." " What will men think when you are out so late? You have a bad name for sheep stealing," says the second. Mak answers that everyone knows his honesty; besides, he is ill—very ill. The third remarks, unpityingly, " Seldom lies the devil dead by the gate." They go to rest, the third insisting that Mak lies between two of them. Mak waits until all are asleep, rises, charms them, and then adds, " Was I never a shepherd, but now will I learn . . ." and makes off with a sheep. He takes it home to his wife and returns to the moor. Immediately, when they wake in the morning, the third shepherd (true to character) reverts to his overnight wariness— " Saw'st thou ought of Mak?" Mak purposely lies sleeping, so that he will escape suspicion. When he is roused, he tells how he dreamt that Jill had another child. He must go. He adds, sarcastically,

> I pray you look at my sleeve, that I steal naught.

The third answers him with a curse.

On the moor, after Mak's return home, the first shepherd reports the loss of a fat wether. "Mak's work," comments the third. "You slander him," says the first, "I saw him go." But the second with considered judgment gives his opinion: in some way Mak has stolen the sheep. "Come on—let's be after him," says the third,

> And run on our feet;
> Shall I never eat bread, the truth till I know.

They return to Mak's hut, where they are at first kept out, for Jill is supposedly ill. But at the first shepherd's polite,

> "Tell us, Mak, if ye may,
> How fare ye, I say,"

the door is opened. The third shepherd goes immediately to the point of their visit—their sheep has vanished. Mak protests that if he had been at the scene of the theft someone would have paid dearly. The first shepherd suggests that he *may* well have been there; the second says that some people might think he had stolen it himself; the third adds

> Either ye or your spouse; so say we.

Mak invites them to search the house. They find nothing. "We made a bad mistake," says the first. "Agreed," says the second, "Your child is a boy?" "A lovely child," answers Mak. The sheep is, of course, in the cradle in place of a baby. "Who are his godparents?" wonders the third ironically. The second shepherd with customary decision asks for Mak's friendship again. Mak tries to hurry their departure. The third comments typically, and still in surly mood, "Fair words there may be, but love there is none." As they go the gentle first shepherd suddenly realises his bad manners. "Gave ye the child anything?" It was only decency to offer the customary gift. "Nothing," says the second. With characteristic irritation and sudden action, the third returns, "Fast again will I fling. Abide ye there." In vain, Mak tries to keep the persistent young man from the cradle. The

M

truth is out. The third shepherd is all for killing Jill and Mak. But the kindly and humorous first shepherd advises

> Sirs, do my rede.
> For this trespass
> We will neither ban nor flyte,
> Fight nor chide.

Instead, they toss Mak in a sheet till they are tired. They return to the moor. An angel tells them of the birth of the true child, and they go to Bethlehem after the wise second shepherd has expounded on the prophecy of David, Isaiah, and others " more than I mind." The view advanced by at least one modern writer that the scene with Mak is a kind of satiric parody of the Nativity tableau which follows—the sheep in the cradle " guying " the Christ child—reveals utter failure to appreciate either the mediaeval mind or the nature of drama in its earlier phases. One might as well say that Aristophanes was trying in the farcical humour of *The Frogs* to undermine the socio-religious life of Athens, when we know he was attempting, if anything, to stabilise it. Just as in Aristophanes, the shepherds attack the abuses of society. Just as in Aristophanes the actors and writer of the play see life as *one* : all is of God, fun, laughter, work, play, all is sacred. Rarely can the folly of looking at a work of theatre from a limited contemporary experience of drama have been so delightfully (and horrifyingly) demonstrated as by the critic noted above. Almost as destructive of the fundamental integrity and nature of this early " comedy " is the habit of omitting the nativity scene in performance. Again, the " modern " mind—so fragmentary in its experience and tentative in its grasp of life —is unwilling to accept what it conceives to be two different dramatic *genres*, or to realise that the profane *is* sacred, and the sacred is concerned with ordinary life, facts so clearly evidenced in the concluding scene. For the shepherds, still in character, do not kneel in sanctimonious affectation, with the stilted sentiment found in some modern religious plays of a popular kind. They bring gifts appropriate and real, as to a child they might know; gifts possible from their own store. The first finds a bunch of cherries; the child smiles and laughs; the second has a pet bird to give the " little tiny mop ". The third brings him the emblem of his own youthful games;

My heart would bleed
To see thee sit here in so poor weed
With no pennies.
Hail! Put forth thy hand,
I bring thee but a ball;
Have and play thee withal—
And go to the tennis.

So they depart. Character is maintained to the last line; the third, the youth, has always been the one to suggest singing—and so—

To sing are we bound;
Let take on high.

His words end the action.

Here then we have much which will later become important in western " comedy ", especially this emphasis on, and interest in, character, the worth of the individual man, which is reflected in our democratic institutions, or so we are told. The " comedy " in Britain and elsewhere gradually loses (in Elizabethan times) its original simplicity. It takes more specialised forms. Popularly, during the eighteenth century, with the advent of a " sentimental " interest in humanity, and lip service to the moral bases of society, it merges into the *drame,* a play of serious intent concerned with individual problems in the pattern of society known to us. In the 1890's and 1900's this is probably most popular on the more fashionable stage—Galsworthy, Pinero, and later, Maugham—all exemplify in their work serious " drawing room comedy ". Sometimes it verges on the tragic—but since its adjustments and " agon " are worked out at the social level it is (if we give regard to the origin of the form) " comedy "; comedy is far from always being " comic " in the popular sense, just as surely as tragedy need not necessarily (even in the strictest Greek classical practice) end in death. Comedy and tragedy, in the west, are derived from two different theatrical approaches, alike, however, in that they are essentially religious in origin.

The student is asked to think along these lines. He may not ultimately agree, and, indeed, so complex a subject, vast as life itself, cannot be contained within easy definition. But at least he may free himself from popular assumptions and dialectic classification. Just as he will be led into a wider world of theatre (if he explores) than the one he has known, so he will ultimately come to recognise that life has many more experiences than those he has met so far, many more than he (perhaps) wishes to recognise. However awkward and annoying it may be, he must face the *whole of human experience* which is reflected in theatre. Examine modern developments in drama in the light of their essential nature and origin.

Tragedy, which dealt from the start with the solemn worship of the God, is concerned with fundamental problems: the ultimate questions of fate, birth, death, struggle, suffering, hate, and love, which will be always there, despite adjustments that any social order can make. And even if the tragic writer has no specific faith himself, his presentation of this basic struggle with environment, the " nature of things ", will inevitably, if he is a great artist, show something of this " nature of things " and reveal some aspect of " religion " in the broader sense. He may see— and not interpret; he may present—and leave us to experience. That, of course, is the character of a great work of art; it has within it life; it is part of the organic creation; it lives in various ways from generation to generation; it speaks in different ways to different people; for it is part of the total human experience and struggle. Something imperishable is caught and trapped there for all time.

Drama evolved from liturgy through use of the myth, which embodied certain lasting aspects of man's experience and struggle. The priests became actors in the presentation of this " myth " which involved in time named characters. It is a characteristic of western theatre that in tragedy it may use ancient stories, often themselves (as in Greek drama) developed myth, and re-exploits their plots so as to demonstrate in some fresh way (especially in French and British theatre) the character and powers of man in his ceaseless struggle for, and towards, life. In *King Lear,* then, an old British story is taken and re-developed. Lear, an arbitrary dictator, demands in old age almost divine worship from those around him. He proposes to partition his kingdom amongst his three daughters—but first they must vie in adoring him; each must say how much she loves him. Regan and Goneril excel in protestations that might make a god jealous. Cordelia refuses—she will love him, she says, as much as she should, no more, no less. (It is the true piety of

Cordelia, her transparent love and sincerity, that activates her refusal to humour the old king. Some modern commentators have blamed her for her unwillingness to act a lie—a strange misunderstanding, surely, of the basis of the conflict in this tragedy, a conflict between truth and falsehood.) In rage the king disinherits her. He will live by turns with his other two daughters. Yet the real situation is shown at the end of the scene when the two evil sisters talk together. Of their father they say, ironically, " He hath ever but slenderly known himself . . ." The tragedy shows the struggle through which he does come to know himself, not as a king, but as a man, to realise wherein the true kingship of humanity consists. So far (the phrase means more to the audience than to the speaker) he " hath ever but slenderly known himself ".

In Shakespeare's *King Lear* there are many statements, as Bradley pointed out, concerning the ultimate nature of the world and its purpose. Such statements are, in accordance with the distinctive approach of western (and especially British) theatre, indicative of character and the part each individual plays in the unfolding of events. Comment, too, varies during the development of a character. Edmund proclaims his rule of life on his entry :

> Thou, Nature, art my goddess; to thy law
> My services are bound.

What he means by " Nature " is gradually made clear. His father Gloucester's attitude is presented in his speech, " These late eclipses in the sun and moon portend no good to us ", ridiculed by Edmund, " When we are sick in fortune—often the surfeit of our own behaviour—we make guilty of our disasters the sun, the moon, and the stars, as if we were villains by necessity, fools by heavenly compulsion . . ." Lear at first, in his anger, invokes Apollo, Jupiter, and begs " Nature " to make his daughter Goneril sterile; then gradually moderates his imprecations, so that when he meets Goneril again, he avows

> I do not bid the thunder bearer shoot,
> Nor tell tales of thee to high judging Jove.
> Mend when thou canst.

Later in the scene he appeals to the gods on his own behalf,

> You see me here, you gods, a poor old man
> As full of grief as age . . .

So we come to the great storm scene when the elements share the tempest in the minds and lives of struggling men, and Lear implores the thunder to

> Crack nature's moulds, all germens spill at once
> That make ungrateful man!

The storm is the disharmony that man has introduced; it is a way judgment may come—inevitably.

> Let the great gods
> Who keep this dreadful pother o'er our heads
> Find out their enemies now.

We return to Gloucester, blinded and fugitive. He seems to have surrendered all hope for any purpose in life; it is for him now meaningless:

> As flies to wanton boys are we to the gods.
> They kill us for their sport.

Albany, when he receives news of Cornwall's death, takes another typical attitude:

> This shows you are above, you justicers,
> That these our nether crimes so speedily can venge.

Kent, the loyal and simple minded courtier, tends (like Gloucester earlier) to adopt a view of acceptance:

> It is the stars, the stars above us,
> Govern our conditions . . .

Yet Gloucester, facing death, prays

O you mighty gods !
This world I do renounce and in your sights
Shake patiently my great affliction off.

He desires that his " snuff and useless part of nature " should
burn itself out.

Opinions, however, do not give us any guide to the interpretation of the tragic theme. They show the views of various characters within the dramatic pattern, and represent some typical
attitudes of mankind. But to appreciate the work of Shakespeare
and its implications we must examine the events, the clash of
action, the basic patterns of human life, therein presented. A
great dramatist does not express opinions; he shows life; it is for
us to share the experience, and to evaluate it as we wish.

A central concern is the way Lear comes to know himself as
man, and then to know what man is. Unreasonably proud,
accustomed to having his slightest whim obeyed, he is at the same
time foolish; he does not know even the nature of his daughters
or the value of those who serve him. So he is easily duped by the
protestations of Goneril and Regan, believes in their love, and
divides the kingdom between them, giving Cordelia, who refuses
to flatter him, nothing except rage. Kent, who strives to direct
the king's thought to something of the truth, is dismissed from
the court. Having given away his kingly power Lear begins to
realise that he has (in himself) very little. First one daughter,
then the other, rejects him. Impotent rage, sheer amazement,
emerge in empty threats. Finally, he goes out on a wild heath as
a storm breaks, alone save for the fool. In words almost too
vivid the " gentleman " tells Kent (still serving faithfully, though
unknown) how Lear

Strives in his little world of man to out-scorn
The to-and-fro conflicting wind and rain.
This night, wherein the cub-drawn bear would couch,
The lion and the belly-pinched wolf
Keep their fur dry, unbonneted he runs,
And bids what will take all.

So Lear has lost all, save " his little world of man ". At first, he
feels that, in this loss, he has abandoned his humanity; he is one
with the lower beasts; but he is touched now with pity for the

fate of his less fortunate brothers; he is beginning to find his real manhood.

> Poor naked wretches, wheresoe'er you are,
> That bide the pelting of this pitiless storm,
> How shall your houseless heads and unfed sides,
> Your loop'd and window'd raggedness defend you
> From seasons such as these? O! I have taken
> Too little care of this. Take physic, pomp;
> Expose thyself to feel what wretches feel . . .

But he has yet to learn that the essential " man " is not found by reduction to the level of lower animals. There comes the most poignant (and perhaps central) moment of the play. Lear meets on the heath a madman clothed in rags. Here, he feels, is the truth. " Thou art the thing itself; unaccommodated man is no more but such a poor, bare, forked animal as thou art." Restrained by the fool, he struggles to tear off his own clothes. " Off, off, you lendings." But the moment of religious awe has come in Lear's question as he looks at the cowering madman and has asked, " Is man no more than this?" For we know then, however marked and marred the appearance of man, there is yet something of eternal value. And with tremendous force, this point is made; for the apparent madman is the disguised and fugitive Edgar, one of the really noble characters in the play. While Lear loses even his reason, passing into a lower world, a hell that he has made for himself, in which everything he sees reminds him of his ungrateful children, whom he attempts to try before a court of justice, a hideous creation of his diseased mind, the human qualities are clearly manifest in Kent and Cordelia, who returns to aid her father. But it would be (in reality) an unhappy ending were Lear to be restored to his former power. He has passed from that to a higher quality of being. Through madness he wakes to a new life, the true love of Cordelia, and even more important, awakes to truth itself.

> I am a very foolish fond old man . . .
> You must bear with me.
> Pray you now forget and forgive; I am old and foolish.

In the battle forces of material power conquer. Lear and

Cordelia are taken prisoner. But Lear has reached a realm where
nothing this world can do will touch him. His speech is one of
the greatest passages in theatre. It would be folly to try to
comment on these words, the essential truth perceived by the
man who has reached, in whatever way, the calm of knowledge
and real wisdom.

> Come, let's away to prison;
> We two alone will sing like birds i' the cage;
> When thou dost ask me blessing, I'll kneel down,
> And ask of thee forgiveness; so we'll live,
> And pray, and sing, and tell old tales, and laugh
> At gilded butterflies, and hear poor rogues
> Talk of court news; and we'll talk with them too,
> Who loses and who wins; who's in, who's out;
> And take upon's the mystery of things,
> As if we were God's spies; and we'll wear out
> In a walled prison, packs and sets of great ones
> That ebb and flow by the moon . . .
> Upon such sacrifices, my Cordelia,
> The gods themselves throw incense.

" And take upon's the mystery of things "; the words repeat
themselves in the mind. Here is the central endeavour of tragedy;
and few plays achieve their end so well as *King Lear*.

Further suffering is in store; but Lear will pass in truth to a
higher life even as he has escaped (in earthly existence) from
material falsities, so that Kent's words are a fitting committal:

> Vex not his ghost. O! let him pass, he hates him
> That would upon the rack of this tough world
> Stretch him out longer.

The insistence on the primitive, almost barbaric, conditions of
life, the savagery; the constant reference to the lower animals;
the ferocity and unbridled desires of characters; all emphasise
the central question, " Is man no more than this?" Even at his
apparent lowest, his kinship with savage beasts, his most
degraded, man's superiority is manifest. Indeed, one of the most
striking features of the action is the way in which negative
" evil " brings positive virtue into being, whether we consider the

servants who decry Cornwall's cruelty or the emergence of Albany as ruler. The touch of truth is shown by Edmund when he is dying. Despite his determined and logical (even cold-blooded) course of self-interest, he cannot maintain his attitude. The spirit within conquers him.

> I pant for life; some good I mean to do
> Despite of mine own nature . . .

His information that he has plotted to kill Lear and Cordelia comes too late.

There are many other elements in the play which we cannot discuss, but here we have one of the greatest tragedies of western theatre. Like life itself, it has its fascinating problems. Judgment is inexorable and automatic; men make their own destiny. We may tremble at the waste of life; we can hardly pity, at times. Even in the last few lines there is matter for thought beyond that normally found in the formal conclusion of a play. Thus Kent refuses to help in the government of the country, itself purged and entering a new phase of existence:

> I have a journey, sir, shortly to go.
> My master calls me, I must not say no.

Commentators differ in their understanding of this. Kent will, it seems, still serve; his lot is bound up with that of the dead Lear. The plays ends with the thought-provoking words of Albany—

> We that are young
> Shall never see so much, nor live so long.

Life is measured by intensity of experience—not by the mere lapse of time intervals.

So the great tragic clash between the forces of the lower life, dragging men downwards, and those of true wisdom which comes from assimilated experience, is played out, centring on the symbolic storm which threatens the very wits, to be succeeded by a tranquillity, light, and peace that pass understanding, at least an understanding which reasons from material considerations.

11. *Summary*

The British theatre shows most of the general aspects of world drama: the persistence of the folk-play, the drama developed from the liturgy of its religion, the establishment of court patronage and court performance, and the effect, again, of the transference of such elaborate and ornate presentation into public theatre, through such workers as D'Avenant. Court influence from 1580-1680 is constant and increasing during a period of activity and change. It might be said that during the reign of Charles II the public professional theatre became itself a Court theatre. When the court no longer condoned its activities or extended its patronage a new challenge faced drama; the rising middle classes had to be won to its support during the eighteenth century.

The "theatrical" costume and conventional décor of the seventeenth and early eighteenth centuries again show analogies with eastern theatre. Afterwards increasingly naturalistic presentation (coupled with that romantic interest in the past which demanded accuracy in costume and setting) developed pictorialism, imported by D'Avenant, until in common with much of western theatre, the attempt to portray the external appearance of the outside world becomes a norm in English theatre. In ballet, however, and to a lesser degree in opera, the more "theatrical" and universal conventions were maintained. We must not forget, however, that even in England the first true "picture frame" did not appear until 1880, and that almost as soon as this became usual (with the idea that the proscenium frame contained a fourth wall which was removed to allow the audience to view), other influences were helping theatre back to more flexible methods of presentation. Cinema, in any case, represented almost the ultimate in picture presentation and the provision of external reality (in appearance) as a background for dramatic action. Here, too, "theatre" intruded; imaginative cutting and emphasis, camera angle and fantasy, restored the basic art forms of theatre. The influence of the east, too, has not been without importance in film. Indeed, western theatre, in all its aspects, is now open to influences from world theatre at large; Britain is sharing in a recovery and extension of mankind's cultural heritage and achievement. Various approaches and theatrical conventions have been blended. The masks of Priestley's *Johnson*

Over Jordan, the simpler décor of Osborne's *The Entertainer*, with its stylised indication of variety stage presentation, space stages, revivals of all kinds of acting areas, from complete arena to apron, show possibilities at our disposal for a creative theatre of the future. A renewed emphasis on music brings back to our theatre a heritage too long confined to musical comedy and the dance routines of variety and floor show, looked on by many theatregoers with disfavour or, at best, amused tolerance. The modern use of music closes the imagined gap, the misleading separation, between " straight " plays and operatic drama. Both are aspects of, and unite in, a greater whole—theatre.

BOOK LIST

Books are listed below as suggestions for further reading, not as a critical bibliography. Further titles will be found in the more specialist works indicated as possible introductions to various branches of a vast subject. Some play titles are included. Works distinctive in style or content, illustrating a dominant trend or innovation, are noted, especially where experience has shown them to be specially challenging or disturbing to students. Accessibility has also prompted inclusion.

General

The Oxford Companion to the Theatre (2nd edition, 1957). Edited Phyllis Hartnoll. Oxford University Press. (Abbreviated as OCT).

A Companion to Classical Studies. Sir Paul Harvey. Oxford. Clarendon Press.

The Oxford Companion to Music. Edited by Percy Scholes. Oxford University Press.

The New Oxford History of Music. I. Ancient and Oriental Music. Edited by Egon Wellesz. Oxford University Press.

Concise Encyclopædia of World History. Edited by John Beale. Hutchinson.

Harvard Dictionary of Music. Edited by Willi Apel. Harvard University Press.

Historical Anthology of Music. Davison and Apel. Vol. 1. Oxford University Press.

Kobbé's Complete Opera Book. Edited by the Earl of Harewood. Putnam.

World Drama. Edited by Barrett H. Clarke. 2 volumes. Dover Books. Constable and Company.

(Abbreviated for reference below as WD.)

The Modern Theatre. Edited by Eric Bentley. 2 volumes. Doubleday Anchor Books, New York.

(Abbreviated for reference below as MT.)

Beaumont, C. W. *Puppets and the Puppet Stage.* Studio Publications.

Bussell, Jan. *The Puppet Theatre.* Faber.

Chambers, E. K. *The Mediaeval Stage.* Oxford, Clarendon Press.

(Still the best general authority for this period.)

Coggan, R. A. *Drama and Education.* Thames and Hudson.

Craig, E. Gordon. *On the Art of Theatre.* Heinemann.

Dent, E. J. *Opera.* Pelican Books.

Haskell, A. *Ballet Panorama.* Batsford.

Laver, James. *Drama: Its Costume and Décor.* Studio Publications.

Lucas, F. L. *Tragedy.* Hogarth Press.

Nicoll, Allardyce. *World Drama,* from Aeschylus to Anouilh. Harrap.

("The present volume . . . is concerned chiefly with the western drama and . . . other kinds of drama are dealt with largely in so far as they have aided in the evolution of western forms."—Extract from Preface.)

Nicoll, Allardyce. *The Development of the Theatre.* Harrap.

Sachs, Curt. *World History of the Dance.* George Allen and Unwin.

Selden and Sellman. *Stage Scenery and Lighting.* Appleton Century, Crofts.

Stevens, D. and Robertson, A. *The Pelican History of Music.* Vol. 1. Ancient Forms to Polyphony. Penguin Books.

(Abbreviated below as PHM.)

Thompson, A. B. *The Anatomy of Drama.* University of California Press.

CHAPTER I

Adam, L. *Primitive Art*. Penguin Books.
Frazer, Sir James. *The Golden Bough*. (12 volumes). Macmillan.
(Also published in a one volume abbreviated version.)
Harrison, Jane. *Ancient Art and Ritual*. Williams and Norgate.
Gaster, T. H. *Thespis*. Henry Schuman, New York
    (Abbreviated for reference below as TH.)
Laming, Annette. *Lascaux. Paintings and Engravings*. Penguin.
For liturgical development see
    Chambers, E. K. *Mediaeval Stage*.
    Pickard Cambridge. *The Dramatic Festivals of Athens*.
    Young, Karl. *The Drama of the Mediæval Church*.
    Read carefully relevant material in *The Sinhalese Folk Play
       and the Modern Stage,* by E. K. Sarathchandra. Cey-
       lon University Press Board.

CHAPTER II

See Canaanite, Hittite, Egyptian, and Hebrew texts (in trans-
lation) in TH. In the same work, study also the analysis of the
Mummers' Play from Stanford-in-the-Vale, Berkshire.
Bouquet, A. C. *Sacred Books of the World*. Penguin Books.
    Comparative Religion. Penguin Books.
James, E. O. *Seasonal Fasts and Festivals*. Thames and Hudson.
    (Chapters in this book, listed below, will serve as introduc-
    tions to the dramatic work of various regions later in this
    handbook, e.g.
       Myth and Ritual in the Ancient Near East.
       The Emergence of Seasonal Rituals.
       The Calendrical Festivals in Egypt.
       Palestinian Festivals.
       The Festivals in Asia Minor and Greece.
       Folk Drama, Dance, and Festival.)
Larousse Encyclopædia of Mythology. Batchworth Press.
Read also, as of especial interest and value, the account of
    dramatic development in a relatively isolated culture, as in-
    stanced by the article on Ethiopia in the *Supplement to the
    Oxford Companion to the Theatre,* 1957 edition, p. 6.

CHAPTER III

Anand, Mulk Raj. *The Indian Theatre.*

Berriedale Keith. *The Sanskrit Drama: its origin, development and practice.*
   (Examine: *Brihâdaranyaka.*)

Bowland, Benjamin. *Art and Architecture of India.* Pelican History of Art. Penguin Books.
   (See especially illustrations of " dancers "—statuettes in limestone from Harappa, p. 3, and copper statuette from Mohenjo-Daro, p.4).

Gopal, Ram. *Indian Dancing.* Phoenix House.

Prabharananda, Swami and Manchester, F. *The Upanishads.* New American Library.

Radhakrishnan. *The Hindu View of Life.* Unwin Books.

Schuyler, M. *A Bibliography of the Sanskrit Drama,* with an introductory sketch of the Dramatic Literature of India. Columbia University Press.

Ryder, A. W. (translated by). *Kalidasa. Various works.* Dent.

CHAPTER IV

Arlington, L. C. *The Chinese Theatre from earliest times until today.* (Contains synopses of 30 Chinese plays).

Chen, Jack. *Chinese Theatre.* Dennis Dobson.
   (Lively and near contemporary account.)

Scott, A. C. *The Classical Theatre of China.* Allen and Unwin.

The Chalk Circle (In WD).

Zucker, A. E. *The Chinese Theatre.* Jarrolds.

Zung, Cecilia S. L. *Secrets of the Chinese Drama.* Harrap.
   (A guide to action and symbolic elements in presentation.)
   Students must remember that it is sometimes difficult to assess the present position and practice of theatre in distant countries. While material may be obtained from Information Services linked with a particular country, only actual " on the spot " observation can (at any given time) be accepted as having real authority.
   See also (for excellent information on the theatre, its conventions, and music) PHM, relevant chapters.

CHAPTER V

Bowers, Faubion. *The Japanese Theatre*. Peter Owen.
Paine, R. T. and Soper, Alexander, *Art and Architecture of
Japan*. Pelican History of Art. Penguin Books.
    (See " theatre, theatre pictures " in the index. Note illustra-
    tions of Nō Masks on p. 95.)
Scott, A. C. *The Kabuki Theatre of Japan*. Allen and Unwin.
Waley, Arthur. *The Nō Plays of Japan*. Allen and Unwin.
    (See, included here, letters and appreciation of the Nō art
    by Sickert.)
Abstraction (Anon.) in WD.
Relevant chapters in PHM.
Relevant articles in OCT.

CHAPTER VI

Aung, Maung Htin. *Burmese Drama*, a study with translation
of Burmese Plays.
Bowers, Faubion. *Theatre in the East*. Nelson.
    (A splendid book of personal observation and assessment.)
Relevant articles in OCT.
Relevant chapters in PHM.
Ni, V. P. *Konmara Pye Zat*, an example of Burmese popular
drama in the nineteenth century.
Sabathchandra, E. R. *The Sinhalese Folk Play and the modern
stage*.
    For shadow plays in Java, etc., see illustrations of such in
    performance and photographs of puppets in OCT,
    2nd. ed., pages 19-22 (illustrations supplement.)
    See also, for history of shadow plays, *Studies in Arab
    Theatre and Cinema*, J. M. Landau. University of
    Pennsylvania Press. Here is interesting cultural affinity
    and interchange between Middle and Far East.

N

CHAPTER VII

Coleman, E. D. *Habimah*. Hebrew Theatre of Palestine. (Tel Aviv).
Duce, Robert. *Steps in Bible Drama*. Independent Press.
(See also, as a study of cultural continuity *Religious Drama* (J. Chapman, S.P.C.K.). Much has come into western theatre from the Hebrew scriptures.)
Frankfort, H. *Art and Architecture of the Ancient Orient*. Pelican History of Art. Penguin Books.
(Notice harp from Ur, and the inlay on the sound box (p. 38); also action and movement on dynastic seal impressions.)
James, E. O. *Seasonal Feasts and Festivals*, chapters II, III, IV.
Landau, J. M. *Studies in Arab Theatre and Cinema*. University of Pennsylvania Press.
Waxman, Meyer. *A History of Jewish Literature*.

CHAPTER VIII

Much of the literature listed below deals with general problems of theatre, and has relevance to eastern theatre as well as western. Since we are a western people our discussion of theatre is necessarily in terms and experiences familiar to ourselves; but these experiences may be seen in, and relate to, a wider context.

General

Aristotle. *Poetics,* etc. Everyman Library. Dent.
Lang, P. H. *Music in Western Civilisation*. Norton and Co. New York.
Lawson, Joan. *European Folk Dance*. Sir Isaac Pitman.
Salter, Lionel. *Going to the Opera*. Phoenix House.
Scarlyn Wilson. *European Drama*. Nicolson and Watson.
Haskell, A. *Ballet Panorama*. Batsford.
Kitchin, L. *Mid-Century Drama*. Faber.
Trewin, J. C. *Theatre since 1900*. Dakers.
Welsford, Enid. *The Court Masque*.

Greek and Roman Theatre

Beare, W. *The Roman Stage*. Methuen.

Lucas, F. L. *Greek Drama for Everyman*. Dent.

Pickard-Cambridge. *The Dramatic Festivals of Athens*. Oxford.

Webster, T. B. C. *Greek Theatrical Production*. Methuen.
>   (Especially valuable for dramatic performance in Sicily and Italy.)

Aeschylus. *Oresteia*. Translated by Gilbert Murray. Allen and Unwin.

Aristophanes. *The Frogs*. Edited, with explanatory notes, by Gilbert Murray. Allen and Unwin.

Euripides. *Bacchae*. Translated Gilbert Murray. Allen and Unwin.
>   *Collected Plays*. Allen and Unwin.

Plautus. *The Captives*. WD.

Seneca. *Medea*. WD.

Terence. *Phormio*. WD.
>   (See also the translations in the Penguin Classics, especially Euripides and Sophocles: *Two Satyr Plays*, Euripides: *Alcestis*, etc., Sophocles: *The Theban plays*.)

Mediaeval

Chambers, E. K. *The Mediaeval Stage*. 2 vols. Oxford.

Halliday, F. R. *The Legend of the Rood*. Duckworth.

Williams, A. *The Drama of Mediaeval England*. Michigan State University Press.

Wickham, Glynne. *Early English Stages*. Routledge and Kegan Paul.

The Mystery of Adam. WD.

Everyman and Other Interludes. Dent.

Chester Mystery Plays, ed. and adapted by M. Hussey, Heinemann Drama Library.

The Ludus Coventriae or *the plaie called Corpus Christi*, edited K. S. Block, Oxford University Press for the Early English Text Society.
>   (Study the introduction for its valuable indication of literary and religious relationships and derivations; note also the developed dramaturgy of these plays and their influence on, and from, the morality drama.)

The Wakefield Plays in the Towneley Cycle. Ed. A. C. Cawley. Manchester University Press.

The York Cycle (Complete edition). Ed. Purvis, J. S. S.P.C.K. (1957).

England

Boas, F. S. *University Drama in the Tudor Age*. Oxford.

Campbell, L. *Scenes and Machines on the English Stage during the Renaissance*. Constable.

Clemen, Wolfgang. *English Tragedy Before Shakespeare*. The development of dramatic speech. Methuen.

Lawrence, W. J. *Old Theatre Days and Ways*. Harrap.

Manifold, J. B. *Music in English Drama*. Rockcliff.

Nicoll, Allardyce. *British Drama*. Harrap.

Rossiter, A. P. *English Drama from Early times to the Elizabethans*. Hutchinson.

> (A valuable and thought-provoking work. " A marked lack of our . . . ' realism ' may be a measure . . . of the more subtle mutual adjustment of actor and audience ". p. 17)

Southern, R. *Mediaeval Theatre in the Round*. Faber.

White, E. R. *The Rise of English Opera*. John Lehmann.

Germany

Bruford, W. H. *Theatre, Drama, and Audience, in Goethe's Germany*.

Gaster, H. F. *Modern German Drama*. Methuen.

von Klenze, C. *From Goethe to Hauptmann. Studies in a Changing Culture*.

Rudins, M. J. *The Origin of the German Carnival Comedy*.

Brecht, B. *Mother Courage*. MT. *The Caucasian Chalk Circle*. (trans. E. and M. Bentley). Oxford University Press.

Goethe, J. W. *Egmont*. WD. *Faust*. Penguin Classics.

Sachs, Hans. *The Wandering Scholar from Paradise*. WD.

Lessing, G. E. *Miss Sara Sampson*. WD.

Schiller, J. C. F. *William Tell*. WD.

France

Chiari, J. *Contemporary French Theatre: The Flight from Naturalism*. Rockcliff.

Frank, Grace. *Mediaeval French Drama*. Oxford University Press.

Hobson, Harold. *The French Theatre Today*. Harrap.

Marsh. E. O. *Jean Anouilh, Poet of Pierrot and Pantaloon*. Allen.

Palmer, John. *Molière and his work*.

Rhodes, S. A. *Contemporary French Theatre*.

Corneille. *Le Cid*. Classiques Illustrés Larousse. *Le Cid*. WD.

Molière. *Six prose comedies* (trans. C. Graveley). Oxford University Press.

Racine. *Berenice*. WD.

Anouilh, J. *Antigone* and *Eurydice*. Methuen.

Giradoux, J. *Tiger at the Gates (La Guerre de Troie n'aura pas lieu)*. Trans. C. Fry. Methuen.

Sartre, J. P. *The Flies, In Camera*. Hamish Hamilton.

Obey, A. *Noah*. Heinemann. Drama Library. (With a valuable introduction by Michel Saint-Denis.)

Italy

Gozzi, Carlo. *Memoirs*. Translated by Arthur Symons.

Kennard, J. S. *The Italian Theatre*, 2 vols.

Starkie, Walter. *Luigi Pirandello*.

Alfieri. *Vittoria. Saul*. WD.

Betti, Ugo. *Six Plays*. Translated by Henry Reed. (Gollancz).

Beolco. *Belora*. WD.

Goldoni. *The Fan*. WD.

Pirandello, Luigi. *Six Characters in Search of an Author*. Heinemann Drama Library.

Scala, Flamineo. *The Portrait*. WD.

Spain

Crawford, J. P. W. *Spanish Drama Before Lope de Vega*.

Gregorsen, Halfdan. *Ibsen and Spain*. A Study in Contemporary Drama. Harvard University Press.

Shoemaker, W. H. *The Multiple Stage in Spain during the Fifteenth and Sixteenth Centuries*. Princeton University Press.

Relevant articles in OCT.

Cervantes. *The Cave of Salamanca*. WD.

Lope de Vega. *The King, the greatest Alcalde*. WD.

Calderon. *The Constant Prince*. WD. *Six Plays*, translated E. L. Service.

Scandinavia

Downes, B. W. *A Study of Six Plays by Ibsen*. Cambridge University Press.

Holberg. *Jeppe of the Hill*. WD.

Ibsen, H. *Four plays*. Edited Desmond McCarthy. Nelson.

Strindberg, A. *Eight Famous Plays*. Duckworth.

Russia

Cooper, Martin. *Russian Opera*. Parrish.

Fulop-Miller, Rene and Gregor, Joseph. *The Russian Theatre, Its Character and History, with special reference to the Revolutionary period*. Paul England.

MacLeod, Joseph. *The New Soviet Theatre*. Allen and Unwin.

Nemirovitch-Dantchenko. *My Life in the Russian Theatre*.

Stanislavsky. *An Actor Prepares*, Bles. *Building a Character*, Reinhardt and Evans. *On the art of the stage*. (With an essay on his system of production and preparation by D. Magarshack). Faber. *Stanislavsky produces Othello*. Bles.

Some suggested reading in contemporary drama.

Eliot, T. S. *The Family Reunion*. Faber. (And other plays).

Marriott, J. W. (Editor). *Great Modern British Plays*. Harrap.

Miller, Arthur. *Collected Plays*. Cresset Press.

O'Casey, Sean. *Collected Plays*. Macmillan.

O'Neill, E. *Mourning Becomes Electra*. Cape. (And other plays).

Osborne, John. *The Entertainer*, Faber. (And other plays).
    A script for television : *A Subject of Scandal and Concern*. Faber.

Pinter, Harold. *The Birthday Party* and *The Caretaker*. Methuen.

Wesker, Arnold. *The Wesker Trilogy*. Cape. (And other plays).

Whiting, John. *Plays*. Heinemann.

Willis, Ted. *Woman in a Dressing Gown, and other television plays*. Barrie and Rockcliff.
    (Valuable preface on *The Writer and Television*).

Yeats, W. B. *Collected Plays*. Macmillan.

Further reading in English drama (general):

The student will find that the compact volumes of The World's Classics (Oxford University Press), collections of complete plays, are the best introduction to any given period. Such are, for example, *Five Pre-Shakespearean Comedies* (with introduction by F. S. Boas) (418), *Five Restoration Tragedies* (Edited Bonamy Dobree) (313), and so on to *Nineteenth Century Plays* (Edited by George Rowell) (533). A recent and valuable addition is *Five Heroic Plays* (Edited by Bonamy Dobree) (576).

Shakespeare

In the following books you will find many of the fundamental problems of theatre discussed, besides the reflection and treatment of these by our greatest dramatist.

Companion to Shakespeare Studies. Cambridge University Press. (See particularly: Theatres and Companies, by Dr. C. J. Sisson).

Barber. C. L. *Shakespeare's Festival Comedy,* a Study of Dramatic Form and its relation to Social Custom. Princeton University Press.

Charlton, H. *Shakespeare's Tragedy.* Cambridge.

Danby, J. F. *Shakespeare's Doctrine of Nature.* A study of King Lear. Faber.

Knights, L. C. *Some Shakespearian Themes.* Chatto and Windus.

Naylor, E. W. *Shakespeare and Music.* Dent.

Ribner, I. *Pattern in Shakespeare's Tragedy.* Methuen.

Spurgeon, Caroline. *Shakespeare's Imagery.* Cambridge University Press.

Wilson, Knight, G. *The Crown of Life.* Methuen. (And other works).

SOME SPECIAL TOPICS IN THEATRE TODAY

EDUCATION: Alington, A. *Drama and Education.* Basil Blackwell.

Burton, E. J. *Drama in Schools.* Herbert Jenkins.

Coggin, P. A. *Drama and Education.* Thames and Hudson.

Lobban, K. M. *Drama in School and Church.* Harrap.

RELIGIOUS DRAMA PRODUCTION AND PLAY LISTS.
  Religious Drama. Edited R. Chapman. S.P.C.K.
RADIO: MacWhinnie, Donald. *The Art of Radio Drama. The Nature of the Medium.* Faber.
TELEVISION: See under Willis, Ted (above). *The Writer and Television.*
FILM: Eisenstein, Sergei. *Film Form: Through Theatre to Cinema.* Dennis Dobson.
  Eisler, Hanns. *Companion to the Cinema.* Dennis Dobson.
  Eliot, T. S. and Hoellering, G. *The Film of Murder in the Cathedral.* Faber.
  Knight, A. *The Liveliest Art.* Macmillan, N.Y.
MUSIC: Settle, Ronald. *Music in the Theatre.* Jenkins.
ACTOR TRAINING: Fishman, M. *The Actor in Training.* Jenkins.
MIME: Mawer, I. *The Art of Mime.* Methuen.
THEATRE AND SOCIETY: Burton, E. J. (Editor). *Theatre, Alive or Dead?* (Statements by Arnold Wesker, Anne Jellicoe, John Whiting, Frances Mackenzie, John Allen, etc.) The Joint Council.

GRAMOPHONE RECORDS

The History of Music in Sound (His Master's Voice), in conjunction with the Oxford University Press, includes in Volume I (Long playing record) excerpts from the following Chinese Operas: *Bair Sheh Juann* (The White Serpent), *Wuu Ja Po* (Lady Precious Stream), the very dramatic *Yuanmen Jaan Tzyy* (Beheading a Son), and *Tsao Chau Guan* (Thatched Bridge Pass). On the second side we have the excerpt from Balinese Theatre, *Tjalonarang.* In addition, there is music such as an instrumental ensemble playing an old dance from Laos and the " Raivo " ceremony with choir and orchestra from Madagascar. The accompanying booklet has valuable illustrations of instruments, ceremonies, and Chinese theatre.

Records of Indian Dance and music are perhaps better known. Western opera is well represented in catalogues. Scenes from Shakespeare are also obtainable. Here we must, however, leave the individual to make his own research and choice.

INDEX

Plays mentioned in the text are not listed below unless specially relevant as illustrative of dramatic development.